ONLY OWLS AND BLOODY F   ...11

ONLY OWLS AND BLOODY FOOLS FLY AT NIGHT

GROUP CAPTAIN
Tom Sawyer
DFC

A Goodall paperback
from
Crécy Publishing Limited

First published in hardback by William Kimber & Co. Ltd. 1982
First Goodall paperback edition 1985
Second Goodall paperback edition 1991
This (third) Goodall edition 2000

ISBN 0 907579 92 2

Photographs courtesy of the Imperial War Museum

A Goodall paperback
published by
Crécy Publishing Limited
1a Ringway Trading Estate, Shadowmoss Road, Manchester M22 5LH

Printed in Malta by
Interprint

Contents

This book is dedicated
To Those Who Did Not Get Back

Acknowledgements

I am grateful to the Controller of Her Majesty's Stationery Office for permission to quote from *Bomber Command 1939-41* published by the Ministry of Information and to W.R. Chorley and R.N. Benwell to quote from their *In Brave Company* and W.R. Chorley's *To See The Dawn Breaking*.

My thanks are also due to my friend Roger Peck for his help in having the typescript prepared. And last but by no means least to Miss Yvonne Doick for the typing.

                                                              TS.

Foreword

by Air Chief Marshal Sir Lewis Hodges
KCB, CBE, DSO, DFC

MANY books have been written during the past forty years describing the work of Bomber Command during the 2nd World War and the day-to-day life of the crews in the bomber squadrons who were faced with the daunting task of carrying out the strategic air offensive against Germany.

Group Captain Tom Sawyer has given us in his book a very vivid and authentic account of what it was like – the relentless work of the bomber squadrons engaged in the continuous round of night attacks against targets in Germany and the occupied territories and the drama and tragedies which faced many who took part. The author served in Bomber Command throughout the whole period of the war, first as a Flight Commander and then as a Squadron Commander and finally as a Station Commander and thus there is no one better qualified to describe the work of the squadrons at first hand and the feelings of those young men who took part – and the majority were very young indeed. In fact, with the passage of time one tends to forget how young they were – the average age in a bomber crew would have been no more than twenty-one years – and yet in spite of their youth they carried out their responsibilities with great fortitude and courage. This is amply borne out in this book.

Tom Sawyer's account covers the whole story of the build-up of Bomber Command from the early days of the war when the training machine underwent an enormous expansion to provide and to train the crews required to man the expanding bomber force. He takes us through the period of the Battle of France and the build-up of the main bomber offensive against Germany and then finally the contribution made by Bomber Command in preparing the way for Operation Overlord and the landing of our forces on the continent.

I had the pleasure of serving under Tom Sawyer in the early days of the war when we were both concerned in training crews in bombing and gunnery and for me this book brings back many memories and it provides another contribution to the history of the air war in Europe during the period 1939 to 1945.

Introduction

BETWEEN the two world wars, military aviation suffered a considerable set-back because of the rapid reduction in all our armed forces, general war-weariness, and then economic recession. The rise of the Fascist and Nazi regimes made little difference until it was nearly too late, because of the unedifying public attitude of appeasement which had overtaken the population except for a small minority, and which was much encouraged by most of our Press at the time.

With virtually no Government investment in research or development, the RAF had to make do for years with wartime aircraft followed by very modest biplane replacements of no real technical advance. However, we did lead the world in our methods and standard of pilot training as developed by the Service, and although World War II started with our having woefully small numbers of frontline aircraft, the RAF recovered just in time to prove that the spirit and example inherited from the old Royal Flying Corps were still there when needed for the defence of our realm.

There was a saying in the RAF in the '30s, when we were messing about with our paraffin bonfires on dew sodden flare-paths in the middle of the night, flogging ourselves and other keen young pilots into the gloom for 'circuits and bumps' or other longer exercises, that 'only owls and bloody fools fly at night'. The following pages are intended to illustrate the truth of that old saying and are therefore mostly concerned with night flying and consequently with Bomber Command. All the anecdotes are quite true, however improbable some may seem.

CHAPTER ONE

World War II Starts

SO it happened that after my two years training as a cadet at Cranwell followed by six years commissioned service in various flying duties, virtually all on biplanes, war was declared on 3rd September 1939. I had recently been promoted to Squadron Leader with a posting to RAF Station Finningley for duties as Flight Commander in a Group Pool Training squadron, oddly enough No 7 (B) Squadron with which I had been flying some five years previously on the clapped-out old Vickers Virginia biplane. They now were equipped with the Avro Anson and the Handley Page Hampden.

At the moment that war was declared, I had the grand total of twenty hours forty-five minutes' night flying as first pilot – mostly on single-engined biplanes. And I was commanding a flight to train embryo bomber pilots up to a suitable standard to enable them to take their places in operational bomber squadrons in the front line. This may now seem rather extraordinary, but at the time was quite normal. My total flying hours were in the region of 1,000 day and night, single-engine and twins, so I was reasonably experienced by then in general terms. Young pilots had still been going into the squadrons with very few hours as first pilot (night), and the wonder of it was that they did so well when it came to the crunch.

With the war started, all this was to change rapidly. Training flying had been stepped up from the beginning of September and continued apace from now on. The night bomber squadrons themselves were fortunately given a chance to bring their crews up to a high pitch of efficiency because of the leaflet raids and the rather slow tempo of the air war at night during those first few weeks. But more of this later.

Much reorganisation was taking place in the Group Pool

Training squadrons, which now had the squadron nomenclature taken away; they were transformed into Operational Training Units, and put under the command of a bomber training group separate from the operational groups, but supplying the latter with fully trained crews after passing through the OTU syllabus. A complete syllabus for ground training as well as air training was worked out and issued to the various OTU stations training crews to fly the Hampdens, Whitleys, and Wellingtons with which the operational squadrons were equipped. And this system remained throughout the war very satisfactorily. The only change was that when the big four-engined bombers came into service later on, the crews from the OTU's went straight into Heavy Conversion Units operated by each of the operational groups to convert them on to the much larger and more complicated aircraft, and the operational groups themselves posted the crews to their own squadrons on completion of this further training.

Therefore, in the middle of September, 7 Squadron lost its identity as a squadron, and moved with all our Ansons and Hampdens to Upper Heyford near Oxford, where the first Hampden OTU was set up. All through that bitter winter of 1939/40 we flew as often as conditions permitted, putting the new intakes through the course, although the weather in December curtailed our flying considerably. At the beginning of March I had to take a detachment down to Stormy Down which was a practice camp in South Wales near Porthcawl, and from where we could use the extensive ranges along Margam Sands for our gunnery and bombing training.

One day I was called out from my flight office to go and examine a Hampden which had just landed back from the ranges after gunnery practice. The tips of both propellers – or more correctly airscrews – had been bent backwards at 90°, all six tips of the three-bladed 'props'. I asked the pilot how it had happened, and he said that he had pulled out of a dive on the final run over the row of targets, misjudged things, and the props had grazed the sand on the beach!

I could see from the expressions on the faces of all the crew that this was not quite the story, so I ordered the pilot to follow me into my office, where I stood him to attention in front of my desk and gave him the b****ing of his young life, and one which he richly deserved. He had of course been indulging in unauthorised low flying, a serious crime in the RAF because of the obvious dangers when a slight error of judgement or badly executed turn could, and frequently did, end in disaster.

I told him that I knew well that his story was absolute poppycock and that he would have been arrested the moment he got out of the aeroplane if I hadn't known that the crew would back his statement at a court martial. I told him that he had been literally only 12in from a violent death and a crash which at over 200mph pulling out of a dive, would have killed the whole crew as well and written off a perfectly good and expensive aeroplane. Also that we didn't train crews for operations against the enemy, for some stupid clot to pile into the British countryside before they could drop a single bomb in anger etc. etc. But I think that he had been shaken more than somewhat by the incident, and realised how close he had been to sudden death, and he left my office looking much chastened, having got the message loud and clear.

The trouble was that low flying was so exhilarating and exciting that sometimes young pilots indulged in it against all the rules and warnings. It was safe enough if you knew what you were doing and kept to above 100ft, which God knows is low enough for almost anyone. But there was always the clot who would go too low, or not see a tree, or mishandle a manoeuvre, and then trouble occurred. My young pupil was damned lucky to get away with his misjudgement. Many a 'famous last word' was uttered as some prune of a pilot 'thought that there was enough room under the bridge'!

We always had to keep one of our Hampdens bombed-up with four anti-submarine bombs while we were there, in case an enemy sub was spotted lurking in the Bristol Channel or South Wales coastal waters looking for our shipping, and one day we received a report that a periscope had been sighted somewhere landward of Lundy Island. So we were ordered to take off and have a crack at it, and with great pleasure amid much excitement the aircraft was quickly prepared and I took off. We carried out a pre-arranged search pattern of the area ordered, but saw nothing for what seemed ages.

Flying at 1,000ft with a fairly calm sea, we peered anxiously for a periscope, and were about to return to the aerodrome in disgust when joy of joys, there it was. A periscope moving through the water making a slight white wash of foam which a speed of about 6 knots would give. Charles Pickard[1] had come along to see the fun, and Sergeant Sheen, one of our bombing instructors/navigator was doing the bombing. Our bombing height had to be 750ft, and the bombs were fused to explode under water at a depth of about 25ft for maximum effect.

Two runs over any submarine discovered were to be made, and Sergeant Sheen directed me carefully over the periscope. 'Bombs gone,' he called, followed by, 'I straddled it'. Good show, I thought, and flew back past the periscope where we saw two black blobs right astern of the periscope which was still moving forward as shown by the white splash of foam. We must have hit it, there were the two patches of tell-tale oil to prove it. So the second run was made, and again Sheen called up, 'Straddled it'. Again the two blobs of oil appeared to be astern of our submarine, but still the periscope ploughed on.

At this stage I began to feel a little anxious, and decided to go down low and have a look. Flying past the object two or three times at 50ft, it became apparent that we had been attacking some sort of marker buoy, and the wash of foam was the tide-rip of several knots which was normal in those confined waters at full spate. The marker buoy itself was

[1]The famous leader who led the Amiens gaol break
and was star of *Target for Tonight*.

hidden below the surface of the muddy waters of the estuary, and only a short, thick stake with a small black flag on top was showing above water, so that the wake created by the tide gave the illusion both for us and for the pilot who initially reported it. From 750ft up it had been most authentic looking, and I had seen periscopes moving through water during my pre-war attachment to the Fleet Air Arm. We couldn't go down to check first of course, in case the periscope was withdrawn while we were messing about. You just have to wade in quickly and ask questions afterwards. I was afraid of much scorn and leg-pulling when we had landed, but no one blamed us or seemed to mind very much, as this had been done several times before by Coastal Command pilots we were informed. But we felt horribly cheated.

During more reorganisation and expansion of the OTUs I was posted to RAF Abingdon, south of Oxford, where I took over the Anson flight of No 10 OTU arriving there on 24 April 1940. This supplied crews to No 4 Group equipped with Whitleys.

The Anson flights at all OTU's were mainly responsible for training wireless operators and navigators in their early air practices, while the pilots were receiving their instruction on the Whitley V to solo standard at night. We did occasionally have the odd pilot in for more dual instruction, day and night, where for some reason they had not received enough twin-engined flying at their Advanced Training School, and this added to the interest of the job as an extra to the normal stooging type of flying we had to do. But it was all good practice for us staff pilots, and we got a lot of flying time in. Some of my pilots were knocking up over 100 hours a month, and I managed to get in sixty to seventy hours a month during that summer for which I was very thankful.

When the pilots were sufficiently capable on the Whitley, the wireless operators and navigators joined their crew captain, and they flew together from then on for the final stages of their training. And it was at this stage that the really tremendous crew spirit was created. Once a crew had decided to fly together and the trainee intakes were left to themselves to pick their own crews from amongst themselves – then that was it. Forever after they only wanted to fly with each other, and when circumstances forced them to fly with other crews, generally through sickness of one of them, then they really did not like it. And therefore when a crew got through a whole bomber tour together – which soon became rather a rare occurrence – it was the same crew which had started together early on in their OTU days.

So the training of bomber crews now became highly organised in all the various aspects of flying at night, and they passed out at the end of the course fully qualified and capable of taking part immediately in bombing operations against the enemy. In fact they were not passed as suitable unless their Flight Commanders were absolutely sure as to their capabilities. But all this was not achieved without some cost, and throughout the course of the war there were many crashes during training for a variety of reasons, and not a few fatalities among them. These were spread of course throughout all the OTUs and having regard to the tremendous amount of flying carried out, were probably as low as could be expected, much research and time being expended on the prevention of accidents. The high standards of instruction both in the air and on the ground also helped to keep accidents to acceptable proportions, and the meticulous servicing and maintenance of aircraft by the technical ground crews was another absolute which inspired confidence in instructors and trainees alike. Not very many accidents were attributable to engine or structural failure.

The actual night flying arrangements were not all that changed, however. Goose-neck flares[2], grass airfields, Aldis lamp signalling, flare-path party out in the cold, and only the Whitleys at last having R/T communication with the ground. At Abingdon, however, there was a Beam Approach

[2]Large oval paraffin containers with a long neck and a wick.

Training Flight, and therefore let into the grass on only one heading – that of the prevailing wind, SW to NE – was a great lighting system of parallel lights forming a landing path. Double rows of bright red at the SW end, white in the centre, and green at the NE end, all in equal lengths. This was not used for normal night flying of course, being far too bright, and really installed for the beam instruction by day. But it came in very useful on occasions when an aircraft was in some difficulty, or to assist operational bombers diverted to Abingdon in bad weather when the lights could be switched on temporarily to show the position of the aerodrome.

In amongst the serious business and necessity of keeping the flow of crews going to the squadrons with the minimum of delay or interruption, in spite of weather or other difficulties, there were a number of more light-hearted moments to enliven our routine, enrich our lives, and otherwise help us to keep a sense of proportion and reasonably sane.

For instance I was OC night flying on one occasion, with rather doubtful weather conditions of low cloud and threatened drizzle. All the cross-country navigation and wireless exercises had been cancelled, but we were still hoping to get a couple of Ansons off on circuits and landings as we were getting a little behind with our programmes. So I arranged to carry out a night weather test myself, before the final decision to cancel all flying was made.

Taking off in an Anson, we were in patchy cloud at 600ft, with 10/10ths at 1,000ft. With light rain falling as well it was obviously unsuitable for even circuits and bumps. It was while we were circling the beacon to take the bearing back to our flare-path, that I suddenly noticed a red port wing navigation light of another aeroplane looming out of the misty cloud close on our starboard side. I immediately started a steep turning dive to port with heart thumping and wondering simultaneously how on earth we had avoided a collision. This had been an instinctive and instantly automatic reaction to my suddenly seeing that damned red light out of the corner of my eye, but I noticed that with my head in a certain position it appeared again, apparently still with us.

In fact it was our orange instrument light which had been turned up too brightly and had also apparently twisted to one side so that it had reflected in the window. A glimpse of this in the black window with some distortion created by the cloud behind it, had been enough to trigger off my reaction. But I had received a nasty shock to the nervous system, and landed a few moments later still sweating from the fright. I must be the only pilot to have taken violent evasive action from his own cockpit lighting. My staff pilots waiting in the flight office all hooted with laughter when I admitted my twitchiness to them!

Not quite as bad though as the pupil pilot who was apparently lost on a dark night on his own, having strayed away from the flare-path. But he then thankfully noticed that a steady red beacon had appeared on his port side far below. But descending in a wide circle from about 3,000ft to 500ft and peering out for the flare-path which he thought should be around somewhere close by, it eventually dawned on him that the said beacon was not getting any larger, and that he had been happily circling his own port navigation light. He got back to his own aerodrome – somehow – and was later mentioned in *Tee Emm* with a citation for the award of the MHDOIF – 'The Most Honourable Derogatory Order of the Irremoveable Finger' – which was awarded to the perpetrator of the worst example of 'Finger Trouble' to reach the editor's desk each month. And, believe me, there were some classics. *Tee Emm* was an official RAF training manual couched in amusing terms wherever possible, and with amusing drawings and cartoons to match. It was much digested and laughed over at all RAF stations, but was a really useful little magazine.

Another hazard at this time after the fall of France and during the build-up to the Battle of Britain, was that on many occasions our aircraft returned to our flare-path after a night exercise only to find that an 'Air Raid Warning Red' was in operation with the Luftwaffe sculling around the countryside making a nuisance of themselves. So we had to push off away from the main aerodrome to a satellite open field where a flare-path was always laid out for just such emergencies. They were also used for practice landings to relieve some of the congestion at the home flare-path. There was only one Nissen hut at these satellites, to house the Officer in Command and the flare party while flying was on, so not much damage could be done if they were bombed, which did happen on some nights since they were a useful decoy to lure enemy bombers.

Much hilarity was caused on one such occasion when one of our staff pilots had been diverted to the satellite flare-path. He landed satisfactorily and parked his Anson where directed by the OC, then he and the crew all ambled off to the Nissen hut for a smoke and a cup of cocoa to wait for the 'all clear' so that they could then return the few miles back home. But a throaty rumble of engines gave the unmistakeable sound of a Heinkel 111 in the vicinity overhead, so they hastily diverted from the Nissen hut to the nearby air-raid shelter, with their pace turning into a gallop as the whine of falling bombs was heard. The instructor was the last to dive headfirst into the shelter just as the stick of bombs was arriving close by, his entry being precipitated by the receipt of a small bomb splinter in his backside with the compliments of the Luftwaffe. The pain in his seat was much less than that to his pride, which suffered greatly at the indignity of the performance.

One of the more classic little moments of history occurred around this time at RAF Station Benson, not very far from Abingdon. This was another OTU at that time, and equipped with the Fairey Battle, a by then redundant day bomber which had suffered great casualties during the Battle of France, but which was still being used for training purposes. After the fall of Poland, a large number of Polish aircrew and others escaped the Nazis, and had been arriving in England increasingly during the fall of France. Many of these were being trained to fly bombers at Benson, and one night a Polish pilot with a crew of two was detailed for a practice bombing flight over the ranges at Otmoor near Oxford, and only a few minutes' flying time from Benson.

However the aircraft did not turn up for its allotted spell at the range, and this was duly reported to the duty officer at Benson. The aircraft should have been back within the hour, and was actually wanted for a second detail later. It did not turn up when expected, nor for two hours after that. And just when everyone thought that they would only hear about the fate of this aircraft and crew when a crash report came in from the police or Observer Corps, the aeroplane arrived. Nearly four hours late, it taxied up to the hangars and the three crew got out all grinning broadly, and highly pleased with themselves. They had decided amongst themselves that to waste eight perfectly good practice bombs of 11lb weight each on the Oxfordshire countryside, was just not on, so they had taken themselves off to Boulogne to have a go at the docks there instead, (where among other places the Germans were assembling their invasion barges) to carry out a private war on their own account. The fact that a practice bomb only made a comparatively small bang, accompanied by a flash and a puff of smoke was immaterial. They reckoned that it would be enough to put the wind up some German soldiery, and perhaps punch a hole through the bottom of a barge with any luck, and that was all they could ask. How could anyone reprimand chaps having that sort of spirit and guts?

One night I was flying a trainee navigator and a wireless operator on a long cross-country exercise to Rhyl and return. We were well on the way on a route I had flown several times before, so I soon realised that we had seen none of the usual aerodrome beacons we should have passed near. The night was very dark, but with reasonable visibility below 10/10ths thick cloud at around 4,000ft so we should have seen the beacons from several miles away. On my asking the navigator for our position, he was not too sure, as the

22

wireless operator could not get any fixes owing to some fault in the set which he could not remedy. (Those gremlins at it again.) Obviously all was not well, and I got a nasty prickly feeling at the nape of my neck. With thick cloud above, the Welsh mountains ahead, and a dodgy wireless set, I decided that discretion was the better part of valour and turned back on a reciprocal course until we eventually sited a friendly beacon and were able to pinpoint our position.

This sort of thing happened all the time throughout the training units, and sometimes a captain would decide to continue for a little longer which might end in a crashed aircraft or a forced landing, and too many aircraft and crews were lost in this way. Flying over blacked-out countryside was very demanding on really dark nights when you could not get above hills or mountains because of too thick cloud. It was all a matter of experience and personal judgement of each captain. I saw no sense in taking risks while training others, and always erred on the careful side, briefing my staff pilots to do the same. There was always another night. The crews were wanted in the squadrons and not in the local cemeteries pushing up daisies. It was a different matter on operations of course, when other considerations held, and the greater needs prevailing made calculated risks acceptable.

At the time of the events which led finally from the so-called Phoney War to the Hot War, and the evacuation of our British Expeditionary Force from Dunkirk, I had just started some overdue leave pending conversion to Whitleys for a posting to an operational squadron which I had requested because I thought it about time I got myself involved in the operational side. But my leave was suddenly cancelled after two days and I was ordered to return to Abingdon immediately. Wondering what the 'flap' was all about, I soon found out, when all the staff instructors were briefed that an invasion of our shores was expected very soon, so we were all to polish up on our own martial expertise while still carrying out the normal training syllabus for the trainee crews. This meant a lot of extra flying, and we all threw ourselves into the task with great zest.

We had gunnery practices for the staff air gunners, with low dive bombing and front gun firing for the pilots in my Anson flight. Formation flying and army co-operation exercises were carried out, and it was obvious to everyone that when the invasion came, all training would cease and we would be thrown into the battle to bomb and strafe the enemy on the beaches, their ships at sea on the way across the Channel, and their assembly points at the French, Belgian and Dutch ports of embarkation. We knew too, that every single aeroplane in the country that could carry a bomb or mount a gun would also be used in order to repel the enemy. We would be required to dô this by day and night, which would have been no picnic for aircraft like the Anson.

In spite of the post-Dunkirk gloom at the turn the war had taken, there was no feeling of despair among us at Abingdon on our little patch there. We had seen the huge pall of smoke towering above Dunkirk, we had taken in some of the remnants of the Air Striking Force from France and seen them bearded and dirty from the retreat, and the surrounding area was full of army troops reforming, equipping, and preparing for the invasion as we were. And our morale was high. We were certain that we would stop the enemy from gaining a beach-head anywhere along the South Coast. And our pride at the recent defeat had been hurt, we were angry and frustrated, but absolutely convinced that the RAF could stop an invasion in its tracks, even looking forward to being able to 'have a go' when the time came. I am sure that the whole of the RAF felt the same way.

So while the Battle of Britain progressed, we reached a high state of readiness with eager anticipation. But the invasion never came and the scare subsided, although not officially recognised as being cancelled for a little while longer, and I was able to renew my request for a posting. This was now possible, and I was duly posted to No 4 Group in Yorkshire on

12 September 1940. But before proceeding up there, some of the developments in the bomber squadrons must be reported to try and show how things had evolved from September 1939.

Of course, while the OTU's had been growing up and fulfilling the training needs of Bomber Command, much more stirring things had been occurring in the squadrons. The Phoney War period had enabled the operational crews to get some valuable and much needed experience of long distance night flying, since most had not flown for periods of more than six hours at a stretch. The famous Leaflet Raids went as far as Poland and Czechoslovakia on occasions, giving excellent training as flights of ten and twelve hours' duration were commonplace. Amusingly, during the first few raids it was found that some of the more distant German towns were fully lit up at nights, because of Göring's boast that no enemy bombers would dare to fly over the Fatherland at all. Needless to say that this state of affairs only lasted for a night or two.

In fact during the first few weeks of the war, this was the only activity in the air over German soil at all. The Blenheim day bombers were sent to Kiel and Bremerhaven looking for the German fleet, and Wellington night bombers were sent out by day a few times also. But the results were so disastrous that they were soon withdrawn from this role, and returned to night flying which was their designed role. Aircraft carried no bombs on the leaflet raids, and Government policy at that time was that no bombing of Germany was to be carried out at all.

Occasionally using aerodromes in France as advanced bases for the longer leaflet raid flights, these extended flights sometimes became a navigator's nightmare. At that time, and for quite a long while after, all air navigation was by 'dead reckoning' on forecast winds and weather only. Unfortunately, the meteorological forecasts were all too frequently incorrect, and large errors in predicted winds and cloud conditions over the Continent were frequent. Lack of facilities and information from Europe was naturally the reason, but this was of no consolation to the crews trying to find their way about over the other side. Astronavigation had not been introduced, and the only external assistance one could get was from W/T Radio Direction Finding 'fixes', or from an actual geographical visual pinpoint fix from ground detail. Both were excellent when they could be obtained, but the ground transmitting stations could not always be 'raised' by the wireless operators in the aircraft as the wireless sets were far from 100 per cent reliable. Frequently it seemed, a pilot would turn round in his seat to look at the wireless operator or navigator who sat close to each other in the Whitley, only to see pieces of the set, or valves, spread all over the W/O's table with him scratching his head wondering what to do next to get the set going again.

Map reading at night was nearly always very difficult because the slightest hint of ground mist or a few patches of cloud, made it impossible to see or identify anything at all of ground detail for a visual position fix to be made. Even on clear nights when coasts, waterways, and lakes could be picked out, the ground between could rarely be properly distinguished even with the use of flares, and again these were hopeless if any ground haze was forming. In bright moonlight things were a lot better if the night was clear, and the Command tended to operate at the maximum during full moon periods if the weather was at all clear, this policy lasting right through to the end of 1942 when our losses in those conditions became too high from the German night fighter force which by then had been built up with a very efficient radar control system to operate it.

The wonder of it was that more aircraft and crews were not lost in the early days of the war through navigational errors. However, it became quite obvious that not only the North Sea was taking its quota, but also the Irish Sea when aeroplanes overflew the country in bad weather having received highly inaccurate forecast winds at briefing, then run out of petrol in due course, not knowing where the hell they had got to.

Leaflet dropping started on the very first night of the war and was carried on consecutively for the next seven nights. From then on they were dropped during the course of normal bombing operations once those had started, and still with great frequency in the first few weeks, sometimes showering propaganda on the Germans, and frequently to give news and hope to the Dutch, Belgian, and French peoples. And apart from the general experience gained by our crews and the Command itself, the aircrews involved got tremendous confidence and experience in bad weather flying. Under peacetime conditions this had been avoided as much as possible, but now some of the raids were carried out in the most appalling weather conditions ever encountered by aviators up to that time.

The Hampdens, Wellingtons, and Whitleys, which were the standard night bombers throughout this period, had got only rather basic de-icing equipment installed, and very inefficient cabin heating systems. The crews had to stuff themselves into their Sidcot Suits with their separate thick woolly 'Teddy Bear' linings, over their own personal choice of polo-neck sweater, which again was beneath a uniform tunic. Sheepskin flying boots and silk inner liners to their flying gauntlets completed the attire apart from the flying helmet with its various attachments and long cord to the earphones. Only the air gunners had the new electrically-heated Irvine Suits and boots, and God knows they needed them. We then waddled – fat and uncomfortable into our aeroplanes and settled down at our flying stations. Once there we were comfortable enough, however, until the cold started to bite in at altitude. What exaggerated the cold was that on top of everything else, the Whitley and Hampden (probably the Wellington also) were more than somewhat draughty inside. With temperatures as low as –30°C logged regularly during that bitter winter of 1939/40, it was almost impossible at times for crews to feel their own hands and feet, let alone to handle their equipment. On one particularly nasty flight at that sort of temperature, one crew reported that the pilot and navigator had banged their heads against the fuselage and chart table in order to get some relief and a different sort of pain to the one they were experiencing from the cold.

Crews also encountered incredibly severe icing conditions for the first time during that awful winter, and they were astonished at the weight and build-up of ice an aircraft could carry yet still be under control. Sometimes even this was over-reached, as there were limits, and the stories of those that got away with it prove that some of the bombers which did not return from some of those flights must have been brought down by ice rather than by the enemy.

One Whitley crash-landed in the dark in France entirely through over-icing. So much was collected that one engine was stopped by it and it then caught fire. The aircraft was forced into a shallow dive at high speed, and the captain ordered crew to abandon but cancelled the order immediately because the rear gunner and wireless operator had both been knocked out by falling equipment in the dive. At a very low altitude the pilot and co-pilot managed to pull the aeroplane just above level as they hurtled out of cloud at only 200ft. There was a dark forest below them, showing clearly for once because of the snow-covered ground, and a lighter patch ahead indicated a clearing into which the captain managed to scrape with undercarriage tucked up. All were unhurt in the landing, thanks to the skill of the pilot, and after putting out the fire in the engine nacelle, they stayed the rest of the night sheltered inside the fuselage of their aircraft. Luckily for them they had landed in France and were helped to a safe return by friendly villagers next morning.

Another Whitley suffered similarly on the same night but fortunately without attendant engine trouble. Six inches of ice formed on the wings, with frost and ice lining the inside of the fuselage as well, and covering all the instruments to make things worse. The controls had been almost locked with ice and chunks were being flung off the airscrew blades to thump ominously on the side of the fuselage. The controls were only kept free by continuous movement, yet the pilot managed to coax the aeroplane home to safety and breakfast.

A third and almost incredible crash-landing was made by yet another Whitley on this same awful night when the aircraft became so solidly covered in ice that the pilot could not move the controls at all, although they were at the time flying at quite a low altitude. The pilot therefore ordered the crew to bale out, and not long after the Whitley came to a slithering halt in open countryside having made a belly landing on its own account.

However, the rear gunner was still in his turret, having become disconnected from the intercom system at some stage and not heard the order to jump. He therefore hurriedly swung his turret round to exit as speedily as he could from the rear, grumbling to himself the while at the b– awful landing his pilot had made. He then wandered round to the front end where he was soon astounded to discover the inexplicable absence of the rest of the crew. However he finally caught up with them in a friendly *estaminet* where the French police had deposited them after rescuing them from various points in the locality. Two of the crew had suffered slight injuries sustained when landing in their parachutes.

Early on in the war when oranges were still available, some were issued on one or two occasions as part of the flying rations. It soon turned out that this was not a very practical dietary offering because they froze solid and could not be eaten until the crews had been on the ground for some hours after landing obviously the forerunner to the modern 'deep freezer'.

Flying rations were somewhat curious at that time and indeed right up to mid-1941, when in 10 Squadron at any rate we were still being given a tube of wine gums or handful of barley sugar sweets, a packet of chewing gum, a small bar of chocolate, and a small packet of biscuits, and, of course, a thermos of hot coffee. It was much better when this odd assortment gave way to great doorsteps of corned beef sandwiches with the coffee, and much more satisfying even though the coffee was sometimes pretty horrible, it was nevertheless always hot and welcome for that alone.

After landing and de-briefing where more tea or coffee was consumed, operational crews always had bacon and eggs for breakfast, and this became an obligatory ritual insisted upon by our Commander-in-Chief later on even when these commodities were hard to get. And who would argue with that? It was much appreciated and enjoyed by all as an aid to the unwinding of recent tensions before going off to bed and sleep. And this special ration was kept up throughout the whole war.

Apropos of this, there was one amusing incident which happened much later on chronologically, but which could be mentioned here. It concerned a certain corporal of the maintenance staff on our station who was one of those dreaded 'barrack-room lawyer' types, always nitpicking and making themselves a nuisance to all and sundry. On each station there was a PSI committee (Personnel and Service Institutes) chaired by the Station Commander, with the catering officer, NAAFI manager, and representatives from each of the NCO's and airmen's messes. It existed to discuss matters relating to the canteen and the running of the various messes, going into ideas for improvements and dealing with complaints etc. Our corporal was making a nuisance of himself as usual at one meeting, and binding away in particular about never having eggs and bacon in the airmen's mess – incidentally neither the sergeants' nor officers' messes served them either since they were particularly hard to come by at that period.

So the Group Captain finally put a stop to the rhetoric by saying quite disarmingly that he might well arrange for him to have eggs and bacon more often if he wanted them so badly. The corporal visibly brightened up at this, thinking that he had gained his point, until the CO added almost as an after-thought, 'That is, if you care to remuster for aircrew duties, corporal.' Collapse of said NCO who was much chastened thereafter.

To return to leaflet dropping, the occasional German fighter had been seen on bright moonlight nights during this campaign, obviously day fighters having a go in clear conditions, but no engagements were ever reported, except one Me109 which approached the tail end of a Whitley just as the navigator was about to dispose of his leaflets down the flare chute. The fighter pulled away quickly without firing a shot however, obviously highly discomforted at being attacked himself by a cloud of bumf.

Apart from the weather and associated navigational hazards, a few other unsolicited excitements occasionally overtook the crews in those early days. For example, the method of disposing of the packets of literature was basic and quite simple. Leaflets were loaded into the fuselage in open cardboard boxes with a given number of packets in each box, each packet being held together with an elastic band. When over the dropping area, the wireless operator, navigator, or rear gunner just had to take out one packet at a time, remove the elastic, and stuff the packet down the flare chute which would be immediately dispersed on emerging into the slipstream.

On one notable occasion, a gunner was arranging the boxes tidily around the flare chute while his aircraft was being taxied out to the take-off point, but being a curious sort of fellow as this was his first trip he decided to take a look at a leaflet in case he was not able to do so later on. So he lifted a packet out of its box and tried to extract one leaflet, but in doing so the elastic flipped off and the whole packet fell to the floor. By this time the aircraft was gathering speed on the take-off run halfway down the flare-path, and the ever present draught inside the Whitley seized the now freed leaflets, and carried them in a fluttering mass into the cockpit, where the astounded pilot suddenly found to his horror – at the moment of lift-off – that his windows were completely papered over on the inside by a shower of pamphlets.

Luckily the instruments were free of the unwelcome deposit and the pilot was able to keep the aircraft on a steady climb while the co-pilot and the navigator frantically peeled off the offending decorations. But it could have been very nasty, and the wretched captain was in an advanced state of shock for quite a while until he had other things to occupy his mind on approaching the enemy coast.

Another different but equally exciting adventure befell the crew of a Whitley returning from a distant leaflet drop over Poland, which being very low in fuel landed in a large convenient field in France in the first dim light of dawn. The motors were switched off, and the whole crew jumped happily out to stretch their legs after an 11-hour flight, walking over to a group of local yokels to ask where they could find a telephone so that they could contact the nearest military or air force unit to ask for a petrol tanker to be sent along. Also, no doubt, they were pleasantly anticipating a visit to the nearest *estaminet* where they could breakfast off fresh rolls, coffee, and brandy while waiting for succour.

After a few moments of conversation, however, it dawned on them with horrible clarity that it was not the friendly French peasantry they were chatting up but some rather amused German counterparts who intimated that the border was but a couple of miles further west, and who also happily expected that the unfortunate British aviators were about to be put 'in the bag'. So backing away as unobtrusively as possible from the not unduly hostile natives, they suddenly turned and galloped back to their aeroplane while at the far end of the field there began to appear a much more sinister group dressed in field grey and clasping muskets to boot, with which they started to take pot shots at the scurrying airmen. After an undignified scramble into their trusty 'kite' to use a well-worn WWI expression – the still warm engines obligingly started up without any hiccups, and they took off hurriedly, ignoring all cockpit drills and all other pre-flight precautions, with a few parting shots from a frustrated detachment of the mighty Wehrmacht zipping harmlessly past. They landed safely again a few minutes later, but really in friendly territory this time.

The leaflet raids continued regularly until mid-March 1940, but they were interspersed with searches for the German Navy which it was optimistically hoped would be caught at sea. Strict orders were issued that no ship was to be attacked if lying alongside a quay or near enough to any land for bombs accidentally to fall on enemy soil. So the Blenheims and occasionally Wellingtons and Hampdens, which were directed against the enemy ships by day, were completely hamstrung when they found naval targets in harbour which they were not allowed to attack. What a way to run a war!

However, obligingly on 16 March 1940 the Luftwaffe attacked a minor target in the Orkneys of all places, injuring a few civilians who were the first British civilian casualties of the war. They also killed a rabbit apparently, a truly hostile act immortalised by Bud Flanagan and Chesney Allen in the hit song 'Run Rabbit, Run Rabbit, Run – Run – Run'. Anyway, this warlike act lifted the inhibitions a little, and the first bombing raid on German sod was carried out on the night of 19/20 March in an attack on the island of Sylt which was a seaplane reconnaissance base where no German civilians lived, and was therefore considered to be a legitimate military target. A raid on Borkum followed soon afterwards, as this was another island air base.

But the Phoney War was soon to be over. Early in April Denmark was over-run and Norway attacked. Bomber Command was able to take up the challenge in real earnest at last. Attacks on enemy-held airfields and shipping in harbours were ordered, and carried out with great determination, although the long sea crossing to Norway and the frequent foul weather created very great difficulties for the night bombers.

The CO of 10 Squadron, flying a Whitley, was forced to

search the fjords at heights between 500 and 3,000ft while looking for Oslo aerodrome. With low cloud and frequent snow showers his task was well nigh impossible, and although at one fjord he found lights blazing and ships unloading at a dock installation, his orders were to bomb the aerodrome so he had to continue searching for Oslo. Not being able to find it under the worsening weather conditions he tried to find the docks again, but a snow storm now obliterated everything and he was reluctantly forced to return to base without dropping any bombs at all after nearly ten hours of exhausting flying.

Another crew, this time in a Wellington bomber, flew down the coast of Norway for almost its whole length at 300ft through frequent snow storms while searching for units of the German navy. It took them fourteen and a half hours flying from Scotland and back in gruelling bad weather.

These were just two examples which were duplicated many times during the short Norwegian campaign of about a month. They cost the Command over thirty crews and aircraft from the small force which was then available, but amply demonstrated that the spirit and dedication of the bomber crews was of the highest order right from the start.

Both the leaflet and the Norwegian campaigns had shown that snow and ice were going to be almost as bitter and frightening enemies to the night flier as were the man-made enemy defences. The contemplation of having to fly through towering cumulo nimbus clouds in winter knowing full well that they would be loaded with ice particles, was as awesome as studying the great enemy defence zones marked out in great red blobs on the giant wall map in the briefing room prior to operations. And when the meteorological officer had given the lurid details of the cloud conditions on certain occasions, showing where the high cloud would be on the way to and from the target for that night, it sometimes created more anxiety among the crews than the bombing operation itself. The aircraft of those days could not get above the bad weather if the cloud was really high, so we just had to plough through it and hope for the best. A so-called de-icing paste was smeared all over the leading edges of the wings, airscrew blades, and prop bosses, with pulsating rubber membranes also fitted to the wings, but these only worked under mild icing conditions and could be swamped by severe deposits.

Then, in early May, the German invasion of Belgium, Holland, and France began, and another phase in night bombing operations was opened up when the tactical use of our night bomber force was called for by the French generals to try and stern the advancing enemy armies. Attacks were first made to the immediate rear of the latest enemy positions in the Low Countries, directed against roads, railways, bridges, supply lines, stores dumps and troop concentrations. But with the fighting being so fluid, a sad lack of up-to-date intelligence coupled with the difficulty of finding such small targets at night, made the help that the night bomber force could give very limited in spite of prodigious effort on the part of the crews. This was not at all the sort of role we should have been asked to undertake, however much we wanted to help the sorely pressed armies. It was much more suited to the day bombers who were coping as best they could with the rather small forces at their disposal. But at long last, on 11 May 1940, the Command was allowed to make its first raids on the German mainland proper, with attacks on railway junctions and marshalling yards from Aachen to Cologne. These operations gave tactical assistance to the Allied armies since they were the direct supply routes to the German forces, and they had the double advantage of having a strategic value as well. This was therefore the start of the long, bitter, and deadly campaign against the enemy heartland which Bomber Command fought continuously and almost nightly, from that moment to the end exactly five long years later.

The Luftwaffe bombing of the centre of Rotterdam a few days later justified the decision to turn on the heat. In order to put an end to Dutch resistance, Hitler ordered the deliberate obliteration of the centre of this undefended city, which was carried out with practice-bombing precision. Like the deliberate massacre at Guernica by the Luftwaffe on Hitler's personal orders a few years earlier during the Spanish civil war. Let those denigrators of the British bombing of Germany please read, mark, learn and inwardly digest. We now knew beyond doubt what we were up against.

In June, with France crumbling and British and French troops beating a fighting retreat to the beaches and western ports, Italy bravely jumped on to the band-wagon so as not to be left out when the spoils of the coming victory were shared out. And therefore Bomber Command was ordered to send a small force to Salon near Marseilles, from whence they could fly out to go and teach Mussolini a short, sharp lesson, with a bombing attack on Genoa docks. It was the only force available to the Allies to take such offensive action against Italy.

So a small force of Wellingtons arrived there on 10 June, but in spite of the operation having been sanctioned by the French Government and High Command, the local area Commander had other ideas and refused to let them take off. The argument continued for several hours, and frequent telephone calls had confirmed to both the local Commander and to our own Air Strike Commander that the operation should take place as planned, and our crews were ordered to take off at the required time. However, as the aircraft were actually being started up ready for the take-off a large number of French military vehicles suddenly appeared and were parked all over the aerodrome to make a take-off impossible, and the operation was aborted.

However, a small force of Whitleys had flown from their bases in Yorkshire, refuelled in the Channel Islands, succeeded in reaching Turin that same night by flying across France and over the Alps, and successfully bombed the Fiat works.

Meanwhile the Commander at Marseilles had finally been forced to allow the Wellingtons to operate from Salon, and they bombed Genoa docks in poor weather on the night of 15 June, also visiting Milan one night later, much to the alarm and despondency of the native population who were both surprised and terrified at this most unfriendly and warlike action. The force returned to England on 18 June when the French sued for an armistice. It transpired that the local Commander for the Southern Region had not wanted the bombing to take place because he was afraid of reprisals from the Italian Air Force! Such was the state of French morale at that time.

After this, various Italian targets were bombed from England on several occasions until late October, and they remained on Bomber Command's visiting list throughout the war for the occasional reminder to keep the Italians on the hop. Their civilian and military morale took a battering as a result, out of all proportion to the intensity of the raids. These trips were always welcomed by the chaps, as they were looked upon as a soft option with a comparatively quiet stooge across France both ways, not much hassle over the target, only a few night fighters to worry about on the way home sometimes much later on, and a stunning view of the Alps by moonlight if the weather permitted. The rotten shooting by the enemy AA gunners over the target usually petered out anyway after the first few salvoes of bombs had fallen, because their intrepid gunners normally hurried off to the cellars and dug-outs themselves once the fun began.

With the fall of France, and the Battle of Britain building up, night bombing at last took on its proper strategic role, when targets like the Krupps works at Essen and other Ruhr manufacturing complexes, the vast Hamm marshalling yards, inland waterways and docks at Duisburg, port facilities at Bremen, Kiel, Hamburg, Emden and so on all received repeated attention as legitimate war targets. And at this stage of the war, crews were always briefed to bring their bombs back if they could not positively identify their main or secondary targets, or find another obviously military target to attack instead. These were termed 'self-evident military objectives' or 'military objectives previously attacked' – known to us as SEMO and MOPA – and would normally be docks and flare-paths. And at this time the crews were really scrupulous in obeying the orders, frequently bringing their bombs back as instructed, but always to their great chagrin.

Any target with water nearby was reasonably easy to find on clear nights even under dark conditions of no moon, but so very often the nights were not clear, when cloud or mist hid water as easily as it hid other ground features. Even quite small amounts of patchy low cloud made identification impossible, and as for Hamm and the Ruhr targets, they were nearly always hidden by industrial haze and absolutely unidentifiable even with the use of parachute flares, which only made matters worse in misty or hazy conditions. Much effort was wasted by having to go back repeatedly to targets which photographic reconnaissance showed had not been damaged sufficiently in previous raids. This was no criticism of the crews who did their best under most difficult conditions, but without really adequate equipment. The targets which were easiest to find on most occasions were of course the Channel and North Sea ports between Rotterdam and Le Havre, where the Germans had begun to assemble vast numbers of barges and small vessels for an invasion of the British Isles.

As the Battle of Britain hotted up, the Luftwaffe extended their targets from the radar stations and RAF fighter aerodromes to sharp attacks on the London docks and then to deliberate bombings of the civil population around the dock areas and to the East End of London generally, causing much damage to civil property and many civilian lives. The first of those indiscriminate raids was on 24 August, and on the night of the 25/26 Bomber Command made its first bombing attack on Berlin as a reprisal, when a suitable military target was selected as the aiming point.

This was an unpleasant surprise to the natives, and a blow to their morale, as well as pricking the ego of the

Reichsminister for the Luftwaffe, Hermann Göring, who had promised the inhabitants that no enemy bombers would either dare – or be allowed – to penetrate that far into Germany at night. Hitler was so angry that he ordered the attacks on London to be stepped up, and these became more and more indiscriminate as the days went by and their air fleets suffered more and more casualties, until 15 September when fifty-six of their number were shot down over England in a desperate two-wave attack to try and finish us off as they had done to Poland and Holland before. And one must not forget the disgraceful attack by a single roving bomber too scared to find a military target, who bravely bombed a small village primary school deep in rural Sussex, killing twenty or thirty infants.

However the Battle of Britain was over as the Luftwaffe had paid too dearly for the previous three weeks, and their losses forced Göring to withdraw the day battle and continue only with the London blitz at night. This became completely wanton and indiscriminate from then on, and later spread to Coventry, Southampton, Liverpool, Hull, and other cities where the town centres were obliterated, without any pretence at attacking military installations or factories producing war materials.

It was at this stage that my own posting to an operational squadron came through, and I arrived at RAF Station Leeming, North Yorkshire, on 12 September 1940 for duties as Flight Commander in No 10 Squadron, which was equipped with the Armstrong Whitworth Whitley V.

CHAPTER TWO

Bomber Ops Early Style

NUMBER 10 Squadron had a high reputation in the
Command, being one of the units which had kept its
identity since World War I and, as with most night bomber
squadrons at that time, the morale was tremendous. The
Station Commander was Bill Staton, who had commanded
the squadron at the outbreak of hostilities and had a chest full
of 'Fruit Salad' (as we irreverently called a collection of
medals) being one of the very few First World War pilots who
had been well decorated then, to receive more decorations in
World War II. He was a huge man and an absolute fire-eater.
The squadron Wing Commander was Sidney Bufton,
efficient and likeable, and by now an experienced night
bomber pilot and a fine leader. I took over from Pat Hanafin
whom I had known at Cranwell, and Charles Whitworth was
the other Flight Commander although he too was awaiting
posting having just been promoted to Wing Commander on
completion of a tour of operations. With a smattering of
experienced pilots still in the squadron, chaps like John
Russell, Tomlinson, Phillips, 'Pinpoint' Prior (a Canadian)
and Steyn (a South African), the unit was in fine fettle and I
was raring to go.

And I wasn't kept hanging around long. The very day after
my arrival the crew to which I was allotted was sent on a long
cross-country settling down flight of nearly four hours'
duration, and later on that evening after we arrived back from
that flight I did a further hour and a half of local circuits and
landings to get used to the aerodrome. Then on the next
night, the 14th, I went on my first operation.

In those days we flew with two pilots, navigator, wireless
operator, and rear gunner. The co-pilot was normally a newer
member of the squadron who had to do half a dozen trips as
second pilot before taking his own crew as captain of aircraft.
Even I as the Flight Commander was told to make three trips

40

as second pilot to get experience under operational conditions, and I was put with a brand new crew, the pilot of which was a very young sergeant who had very recently come from OTU and had just finished his obligatory few trips as second dicky. I must admit to being a trifle nervous at the prospect of being second 'joe' to a bit of a sprog, but there it was. It had to be done.

We were detailed for a 'barge bashing' trip to Antwerp, because the enemy invasion fleets were still assembled although the danger of them being used had receded by now. These therefore were still on the programme, and quite enjoyed by all, because they entailed a quick dash over the enemy coast and back without hours of stooging over blacked-out enemy territory. Good weather was always chosen also, because all the ports were in occupied Europe and we needed to be able to see what we were doing in the way of target identification. The targets themselves were not all that easy though, as the Germans had assembled masses of searchlights and light flak guns to defend their soldiery and ships, and put up a very hostile reception whenever we made an appearance overhead. Still, they were useful trips for new crews to gain experience on. And I will never forget this one.

On the way out I said that I would do the actual bombing as I did not want to be a complete passenger, and the navigator, who normally did the bomb aiming, came forward to check that my settings of the bomb sight were correct. We could see the activity over the target from a long way off as it was a lovely clear night, and I watched our approach eagerly from down in the nose lying in the prone position. We were to drop two sticks of bombs in two runs over the target from 8,000ft, the aiming point being the centre of the dock area.

There was much searchlight activity with several aircraft obviously in the vicinity, and on our run-in a great increase in the amount of light flak tracer which seemed to be sprayed up all over the place almost indiscriminately and in all directions in prodigious quantities. Multicoloured strings of orange, red, and even green were hosed upwards, sometimes with a sort of 'S' bend in them as the gunners swung their barrels around. White and yellow blobs of fairy lights creeping up almost lazily at first, then with gradually increasing velocity to zip past the wings at terrific speed, and some a little too close for complacency. There were our old friends from World War I – the 'Flaming Onions' soaring up in small strings of five angry red or orange balls. The whole panorama criss-crossed in an untidy mêlée yet somehow almost beautiful, as I pored over the sights giving the pilot the directions. 'Left, left – steady – right a bit, steady' etc.

The whole target area was clearly visible and a strangely exultant feeling welled up inside me as I got ready to let go the first stick, chuckling like a maniac as I did so in my excitement. I turned round quickly on the floor, asking the pilot to keep going straight ahead while I lifted the floor escape hatch to try and plot the fall of our bombs. But in the welter of twinkling lights, gun flashes, and small fires, I could not make out our bomb falls.

'Just like a Brocks Benefit Night,' I called to the crew as I steered the pilot on to our second run.

I pressed the bomb tit for the second time and raised the floor hatch again while we flew straight ahead. And this time I got them. Peering anxiously downwards and slightly backwards I saw four lovely flashes appear in a line right across the docks. A bullseye. Three flashes from the basin where the barges were berthed, and one on the dock-side itself. I slammed the hatch shut and asked the pilot if he would make a circuit of the whole area so that I could watch and report on the results generally. Then we headed for home. I was light-hearted, light-headed even, and happy to be in amongst the action at last. I have still got the target map issued that night, with the four bomb bursts marked in pencil at the time where I saw them explode.

It may seem strange to bomber types of later years that we were only at 8,000ft, but that was fairly standard at the time although earlier on heights of 4–5,000ft were normal. This was considered about right for the effectiveness of light flak, although on that night it was whipping past us to greater heights. And as the enemy raised the heights at which light flak could be lethal, so our bombing heights were pushing higher and higher until only above 14,000ft could we feel safe from light flak. By then we were in the heavy flak zone anyway, so we just had to put up with that, and bombed from 15–18,000ft thereafter.

So by now our bombers were cruising all over Western Germany more or less every night in small numbers, and when the main target could not be found during the thirty minutes or one hour we were usually given on each target to find it, the crews would then have to look round for a 'Semo' or 'Mopa'. Many were the surprised and indignant members of searchlight or flak batteries who suddenly received a parcel of bombs from a browned-off British bomber crew who hadn't been able to find any more suitable target before crossing the enemy coast on the way home. And consequently on occasions in certain weather conditions we were not challenged at all, as the ground defence seemed to realise that we were browsing around quite unable to find what we were looking for, and how right they were. By the end of December 1940 we had become less careful, and no one ever brought bombs back. We remembered the London blitz, Coventry, Southampton, and Liverpool which were very fresh in our minds.

The practice in those days, and one which lasted well into 1941, was that after Command had given the Group Commanders their targets for the night – it was usually two or even three, and different for each group – these would then be allocated to whichever station was picked for operations that night since it would not necessarily be all of them. At least one station in each group was on stand-down every time. The Station and Squadron Commanders would then work out their own flight plan, picking their own choice of route, heights, and time on target irrespective of what the other stations were doing. Some squadrons preferred to take off at dusk and land back in the dark, others conversely liking a dawn landing with a night take-off, but always subject to their own interpretation of the Met forecasts as relayed down from HQ at High Wycombe. So of the 50-odd aircraft which could be mustered in any one group every night, not all of them would be called upon in the first place, and even these might be spread between two targets. It was therefore quite normal for only eight or ten aeroplanes from one squadron to be attacking a target at any one time. If it was at any distance or visibility of the ground was bad, there would be a small number of aircraft milling about the German countryside quite alone over a wide area.

This may seem strange in the light of policies which evolved later, but this was still in the very early phase of the bombing war, and we were in the process of development of tactics with a small force and a huge area to cover. And it did have one great asset in that the sirens would have been going all over Western Germany and all through the night as well, giving the natives sleepless nights on most nights and over very large areas considering the strength available. Single bombers would be cruising around on their own because of navigational differences, and adding to the areas under alert. There were virtually no enemy night fighters to harass us at that time, so that this thin spread was possible, until mid-1941 when the Germans were beginning to develop a night fighter force with the necessary ground control organisation to operate it, the old sound locators giving way to radar. But by then we had more bombers to employ as the Command was steadily, if slowly, growing. The theory of bomber safety being improved by concentration of effort was also beginning to develop by then.

Another classic example of the difficulties of navigating by dead reckoning only and forcefully demonstrating how easy it was to go astray, occurred one night in the late summer of 1940 when a crew had been detailed with a few others to bomb a target in the Ruhr. Ground visibility was poor crossing the sea, and no pin-point could be made over the Dutch coast on the way out. Thick haze also obscured the target area as usual and in spite of searching for an hour after ETA, dropping flares in a square search, absolutely nothing could be seen. To make matters worse the wireless operator could not raise the D/F stations to get a fix, so reluctantly they turned for home hoping to find a Semo or Mopa on which to deposit their cargo on the way back. But the natives were having the good sense not to interfere and no guns opened up on them. Then sure enough, a break in the ground haze and mist suddenly disclosed a flare-path conveniently laid out for their attention, which they took from the navigator's calculations to be somewhere in Holland.

Apart from this, they still saw nothing of coastal detail or British beacons all the way up England and on ETA Base duly called up flying control on R/T for landing instructions. But answer came there none. Then suddenly and most fortuitously, the gremlins, who had been inhabiting the wireless set for the whole trip so far, decided they had had enough fun, and it came to life allowing the W/Op to get a first class fix which showed them, to their utter astonishment, to be over the Irish Sea. They finally arrived back at their own aerodrome some two hours later bemused but safe.

On going over their charts the next morning with the Station Navigation Officer, and using the true winds as found by other crews that night, it became apparent that they must have dropped their bombs somewhere in East Anglia. The forecast winds had been well out, and they had not been able to check their position *en-route* either by visual identification or by W/T. And sure enough, when Group checked with Command after this was reported to them, it was learned that RAF Station Bassingbourn in Cambridgeshire had received a very unwelcome stick of supposedly enemy bombs at the exact time the navigator had logged his own time of bombing. Happily only a string of craters was made in the grass aerodrome, and a shocked corporal was dislodged from his bunk in the D/F hut on the edge of the airfield by the blast of the last bomb in the stick, disturbing his pleasant dreams but causing him no more harm than a certain amount of alarm and despondency. No doubt he quickly recovered and became the hero of the corporals' mess for a week or two afterwards.

From about April 1940 onwards another task allocated to Bomber Command as well as to other Commands, was that of laying acoustic and magnetic mines in the coastal shipping sea lanes around Europe. From the fjords of Norway, all round Denmark, into the Baltic, along the north-west coast of Germany facing the North Sea, the estuaries of Holland, to the coastal waters of France, the dropping of these mines from the air continued frequently if spasmodically throughout the war. And highly successful they were too, causing much disruption to enemy shipping, and sinking many vessels of all descriptions.

At first the Hampdens of No 5 Group were specially adapted to carry out this work, but it was eventually done by all groups and involved low flying over the sea in order to drop the mines successfully. Most crews rather liked this particular job, partly because it was a bit different from the normal and long flights over the sea were preferable to long stooges over enemy territory. But they were by no means a piece of cake, and could be somewhat dicey at times because the enemy soon started to put flakships in their estuaries and sealanes. Bristling with anti-aircraft guns of all descriptions, including multiple pom-poms which were very nasty heavy calibre quick-firing weapons called by our Royal Navy 'Chicago Pianos', a crew flying at about 300ft would be suddenly engaged at close quarters out of an apparently empty sea, by a selection of angry, quick-firing artillery pieces, which at those low altitudes and close ranges was most unpleasant and frequently lethal. Later on when the four-engined bombers could carry bigger and better mines, these were parachuted down from somewhat safer altitudes of 3-4,000ft, although this too could be a bit dodgy if one got too close to a flakship or strayed over a coastal battery.

Following on Antwerp, I went to Hamburg and Soest in quick succession and still as co-pilot with my young crew. At Hamburg we were after the great battleship *Bismarck* which had been photographed in dry dock there. We found the mouth of the Elbe quite easily on a dark but clear night, and followed the river down to the port of Hamburg, being shot at by heavy flak this time all the way in, much to our discomfiture. The Germans had of course realised that this was the best way for us to find this target, and, with Brunsbüttel and Cuxhaven at the mouth also needing protection, had lined the whole estuary with flak batteries along the complete stretch to Hamburg. So we had an unfriendly reception during the 55-mile approach – which at 130mph takes no mathematical genius to work out as being twenty-eight minutes of absolutely personal attention from the extremely hostile natives.

Over Hamburg itself, the flak remained undiminished while much searchlight activity was added. I was dropping the bombs again, and could see no ground detail at all now that the river had narrowed into the town, and there was also a very wide smoke screen which had been added to the normal industrial haze of a large town. As our instructions were that we must only bomb if we could identify the target positively, I called to the pilot to continue straight over the area and turn to port so that I could look for an alternative, having some of the flak batteries in mind. But luckily I saw some aerodrome lighting and a flare-path laid out at Shillighorn, and was able to dispose of our load there.

Soest was a large marshalling yard east of Hamm, and having flown over large amounts of cloud, just below us we arrived at the target area in clear enough weather, but again with much ground haze which completely baffled our parachute flares so that I could distinguish no ground detail. We had received two good fixes *en-route*, so knew where we were when on ETA we received a fair amount of attention from the ground defences. So I let the bombs go at a group of searchlights where gun flashes were also to be seen. The yards were well out in the country anyway, away from the built-up area.

On the way home, however, we found that the cloud had built up most unpleasantly and we had to plunge right into huge, towering banks of cumulo nimbus which we could not get above, and immediately the aircraft began to be tossed around quite alarmingly in the bumpy conditions. I was sitting beside my sergeant pilot metaphorically biting my nails with anxiety as I watched the turn and bank indicator and the artificial horizon, on the instrument panel gyrating madly in all directions, with the direction indicator and gyro compass swinging to and fro in the dreadful lurches the poor lad was trying in vain to control. I wanted to take over immediately, but he was officially the captain, and for the sake of his self-esteem I held back – albeit anxiously.

Luckily however – if you can call it so – he very soon began to pass wind every few seconds through fear, filling the cabin with noxious fumes, and I realised thankfully that he was even more terrified than I was, if that were possible, and that if I didn't take over soon we would be in a spin any moment now. So I suggested quietly that he might prefer me to drive and he agreed with alacrity, changing seats with me in record time.

We had only been in the cloud for a couple of minutes but were almost completely out of control from the moment we had entered it. I quickly got the aircraft steady and back on course, showing him that there was really not much to worry about in cloud unless it brought on heavy icing with it. We had none of that at all I'm glad to say, and I even put 'George' on to fly for a spell to give him added confidence.

George was the RAF terminology for the automatic pilot system built into every heavy bomber, and it was extremely reliable. Now and again if it was in action over a long period the gyro might topple, and some dramatic manoeuvre would result which necessitated instant re-action from the captain to switch it off and recover attitude manually. Even this was very infrequent. But of course George only flew straight and level which was not to be recommended at any stage over enemy territory for any length of time, even in those far off days, because predicted flak could come uncomfortably close if an aircraft had been flying absolutely straight and level near a defended area for more than a few minutes. I never used George very much myself, always preferring to do all serious instrument flying for personal enjoyment and practice. Only occasionally on long stooges over the North Sea where it was completely safe to fly level for long periods, would I cut it in for a spell.

I sent my sergeant pilot next day to the Link Trainer Instructor with orders to be given ten hours under the hood as quickly as possible, at least five hours of which must be under simulated bumpy conditions. He was completely confident in cloud after all that, but sadly only a few weeks later he flew into a balloon cable over Brooklands in poor weather returning from a sortie, and all the crew were killed.

I was now allowed to take an aeroplane and crew as a captain, and three nights later went to Boulogne as a settling down trip on another barge-bashing expedition. A short trip, but with only two or three other aircraft on the same target we received a very healthy welcome, and for the second time I heard heavy flak bursting at close quarters. This always sounded as though a giant fist was pounding against the outside of the fuselage, and you knew then that it was getting a little too close for comfort. But we only received a few small shrapnel holes which did no real damage.

This was followed the very next night by a long stooge to Frankfort-on-Oder just the other side of Berlin, with the secondary target being the Siemens Works on the fringes of the Big City itself. We always called Berlin by this throughout the whole war in a kind of reverse endearment or love/hate sarcasm, from the very first bombing attack in August 1940 to the bitter battles over the city in '43 and '44 and on to the end. However, on this night the ground detail over the target was obscured by mist and we turned back to Berlin to look for the secondary. Luckily one of our flares eventually showed up the large lake on the west side of Berlin, and we were able to 'lay off' on a timed run from there to bomb the Siemens works. Apart from being my first really long distance flight – it took over ten hours – the sortie was memorable to me for two other reasons. Firstly while we were circling around the target area trying to identify some ground detail in the light of our flares, I had opened the sliding window beside me to get a clearer view and was peering hopefully downwards, when I realised that the controls were getting a trifle sloppy.

Looking down quickly at the instruments, I found that we were in a steep climbing turn with the airspeed indicator below the 90mph mark while still rapidly unwinding. I just managed to stuff the nose down before a spin developed, straightened up at the same time and all was well. Good old Whitley V, any other aeroplane would have spun long before that. It was not all that dangerous though since a spin from 14,000ft would have given plenty of space to recover in, even with a full bomb load. But it taught me that I would have to be more careful in future when goofing over the side looking to see where we were. I had been so engrossed in that to have quite forgotten to think about the attitude of the aeroplane. Part of the trouble was that there was absolutely no horizon visible, and no stars either, which were obscured by a very high thin layer of cloud. A completely dark, black night resulted.

The second interesting feature of that night's operation was that because of the distance involved we had been briefed to land back at Great Massingham, in Norfolk, a satellite flare-path to West Raynham. We crossed the Suffolk coast in the right place, and soon saw several aerodrome beacons flashing away merrily. This was always a marvellous moment when it happened. Having the English coast come up on track and then seeing all the various beacons winking their welcoming messages was really satisfying. Unfortunately it didn't seem to happen that way very often! At this time, the airfields in East Anglia had been receiving much unwelcome attention from enemy intruders. Consequently they had to limit the amount of light they could show, and could not use the normal gooseneck paraffin flares which could be seen for miles from every direction on clear nights. They therefore used the more modern and less bright 'glim lamps' instead. These were a sort of large torchlight bulb run off a dry battery and set in a vertical cylinder about 12in tall and 8 or 9in diameter. They had a glass domed top and a wide-angle reflector which did not cast a beam. Seen from above they only gave a pinpoint of light, and could not be seen at all from above 2,000ft. And in East Anglia, not only did they use these, but covered them over with a metal shroud as well, so that the lights could only be seen from one narrow direction. You had to fly to the aerodrome beacon – each one having its own letter to identify it, and the code for which was frequently changed – then set course for the flare-path on a predetermined heading for about ten miles or whatever similar distance it happened to be, then you had to locate the glim lamps by circling round until you found the narrow gap which you obviously had to be down-wind of. All very fraught, and pilots had to go back to the beacon two or three times on some occasions before the glims could be found. Not very funny after a long stooge. It was bad enough having to do this on a clear night, and how the crews operating permanently from East Anglia managed it night after night I shall never know.

So with an attack on the submarine pens at Lorient before the end of September, I had notched up a useful six operations in the fortnight I had been on the squadron strength, and I had visions of getting through my tour quickly in seven or eight months or even less with any luck. But various things occurred to upset my hoped for timetable, to interrupt and prolong it for another fifteen months. The autumn and winter months were rainy and wet, and the airfield was turned into a quagmire, the grass between the dispersal areas becoming a soggy mess. Then when once a Flight Commander had 'got some in', as the saying went, he did not fly as often as the junior crews, and still had to get through the quota of thirty operations. An experienced Squadron Commander flew even less often, as with the Command now beginning to expand it was imperative to keep the key personnel in the squadrons for as long as reasonably possible. And finally, when I had completed some twenty odd sorties, I was posted away to form and train a new squadron at Linton-on-Ouse where the latest huge four-engined Halifax bombers were being allotted to two squadrons. These and the Short Stirling were the first of the new generation of heavy bombers with which the Command began re-equipping from April 1941.

The Lorient trip was successful as far as the journey out to the target was concerned, but on the way back, at the time we should have been over the Oxford area and seeing a few flashing beacons, all I could see when I looked down through my window was part of a jagged coastline. We should have cleared the Brest peninsula and the Brittany coast an hour before, and it certainly wasn't Southampton Water and the Solent we could see through about 3/10ths cloud. So I asked my navigator where the hell he thought he was taking us, and a convenient W/T fix the wireless operator produced for us at that moment, showed that we were over the Gower Peninsular – West Wales. So we turned due east and headed for Abingdon where we landed safely. My navigator was Pilot Officer Beeston, a Welshman, and I told him that next time he felt the urge to adopt the instincts of a homing pigeon and return to his native hills, would he kindly inform me first so that I would know what to expect.

A couple of days later, the squadron visited Berlin again,

and we lost two aircraft out of the nine taking part. One was last heard calling for a fix over north-west Germany – and then nothing more. The other suddenly called for a fix at 04.43 hours when they were well overdue, and this put the Whitley miles out over the Irish Sea having overshot England. Whether they received the fix it was impossible to say, but they were heard again one hour later when they broadcast an SOS which meant that they were about to ditch in the sea. The whole crew were picked up unhurt by a trawler which luckily had been fairly near to them, and they were landed at Holyhead some twelve hours later and taken into hospital, all suffering from shock.

My next sortie somewhat dented my self-esteem and confidence, as it turned out to be a horrid example of 'finger trouble' plus gremlinitis with a little bit of 'prunery' thrown in for luck. I have already briefly mentioned the legendary Pilot Officer Prune, who was the archetypal RAF clot, always in trouble, never obeying flying rules or regulations, never studying his manuals or reading orders, and therefore cheerfully pranging aeroplanes all over the place through sheer stupidity and neglect, but nevertheless always getting away with his awful errors more or less unharmed. I am ashamed to have to admit to some part in this event because I must acknowledge responsibility in certain respects. And I do so in order to illustrate that odd things did happen to the reasoning faculties of otherwise fairly sensible bods who were not normally prone to getting in a flap. If a certain amount of pressure after some unusually dicey situation had used up their normal supply of adrenalin, this sometimes hampered the usual thought processes.

The target was a synthetic oil refinery situated just south of Cologne on a sharp bend of the Rhine. The night was clear but dark, and the outward flight was dead on track all the time bringing us on the run-up to Cologne with the river clearly visible from 10,000ft. The navigator was down in the nose making the preparations for our bombing run, and just as he was about to start giving me the necessary heading corrections, the twenty or so searchlights which up to that moment had been weaving slowly about without much apparent co-ordination, all swung over towards us as one of them picked us up in its beam, and solidly fixed on us personally. And there we were, coned, that dreaded word which had started to creep into the bomber crew's vocabulary in the messes, crew rooms, and at briefings.

The German ground defences had been building up rapidly since the fall of France when our aircraft had started to roam nightly over the Fatherland at will, and by the autumn of 1940 were showing extreme hostility in many areas, and particularly at all major target towns where they had the good sense to concentrate their searchlight and flak batteries. Several reports of aircraft being coned had been passed round the Groups and to the squadrons, giving rise to much discussion amongst the crews as to the best way to deal with such an event if it happened to them personally. One Wellington pilot had reported that he had escaped from such a situation by stuffing the nose down and diving out of trouble at speed, and it was generally thought then that perhaps this was the best way.

So now being on the receiving end of the undivided attention of all the Cologne area defences, and being personally subjected to the heaviest concentration of searchlights and flak I had yet encountered, I remembered the report of the Wellington crew, pushed the nose down and dived sedately away from the hornet's nest we had wandered into. Sedately, because the Whitley's cruising speed of 130mph hardly allowed of much more although it did build up to 230mph on the clock. At this speed the wings appeared to be flapping and the controls were absolutely rigid and solid. The searchlights and flak followed us down easily enough of course, the heavy stuff being joined by light guns as we got lower and much tracer whipping past us on both sides as the rear gunner gave a squirt or two at the nearest searchlights.

Eventually all the tracer came horizontally from behind as we started to pull away from the area and I flattened out of the dive heading south, and still going like the clappers, drawing away from the defences finally at 1,000ft.

We still had our bombing run to do of course, as all this had rather put us off that for the moment, so I used up our excess speed to regain some of our lost height, and told the crew that we would get back to our bombing height in a long sweep to make our run from south to north. The navigator was still in the nose, and the crew had not uttered a word all the time. I found that I was sweating and that my mouth was absolutely dry, but I made the wide detour climbing as fast as possible, and keeping the Rhine in sight all the while.

The bend in the river could still be clearly seen where the target was situated, and as we ran in we were subjected to more heavy flak which although somewhat disconcerting was happily not all that accurate, and immediately I got the 'Bombs Gone'. I turned hard to port to avoid the Cologne searchlights, and then back on a northerly course for home. I cannot remember now if I pulled the master toggle for manual release of the bombs which was the normal drill in the Whitley and a safeguard against electrical failure of the bomb mechanism, but if I didn't it was because I was pre-occupied with the bursts of heavy flak which were appearing in our direction during this second attempt at the target.

We did not get a pin-point crossing the Dutch coast as ground mist had developed, but we droned quietly on northwards, each of us busy with our own jobs and thoughts, and I did not feel the slightest worry until the time we should have been arriving over Flamborough Head, although we should have seen the odd beacon as we skirted the East Anglian coast. I put this down to ground mist as the night was clear enough otherwise. I asked the wireless operator to get a fix for the navigator and sent the second pilot back to drop flares down the chute, but we could see nothing. I turned off our northerly course and flew due west to try and make a landfall, but after about twenty minutes' flying with no land appearing I started to get the horrible fear that we had overshot England and gone out into the Irish Sea as the two others had done quite recently before. The navigator could offer no help, and I asked about any fixes, telling the wireless operator to keep trying and turning east again as I was now convinced that we were over the Irish Sea.

A pale dawn was beginning to come up by now, and we were long past our ETA base. There was nothing but water below and the mist had lifted with the coming day. Several times we were lured towards dark shadows low on the horizon believing it to be land, but only to find that they turned out to be low banks of lifted mist. The navigator said that he could not make out the fixes he had been given, and had no idea where we were. After messing about like this for what seemed ages, my mind which had been stupefied and almost numb for well over an hour, suddenly cleared and I came to again, deciding that we still had enough petrol to make Northern Ireland even if we were that side of England. In the light of the weather conditions I now doubted this, since the mist had obviously not been dense enough to blot out all beacons if we had been flying over land before.

So I turned due west again and held grimly on to that course, and sure enough after half an hour a long dark line on the horizon heralded the land and soon Scarborough Castle showed up dead ahead. A small alteration of course took us to Leeming, where we landed nearly three hours after everyone else. A quick examination of the fuselage as we got out of the aircraft showed that we had about thirty holes of various sizes received from shrapnel and small bore machine guns, so at least we had something to show for our pains. But on our arrival in the ops room to be de-briefed, the wall map showed at least six first-class fixes in a group about 60 miles out to sea off the Yorkshire coast. Our wireless operator had received them all, and passed them to the navigator, who had disregarded them without plotting them on his chart. It seemed that the pasting we had received before bombing, and again on our second run over the target, had been rather too much for him and he had mentally frozen from then on. He was a quiet, pleasant chap and a school master in normal times, and a little older than the rest of us.

The intelligence officer was half way through our debriefing interrogation when a message came through from the flight that all our bombs were still on board. After all that, and a perfect run up to a target we could plainly see for once so easily! It was too much. I don't know why the bombs did not go, because the navigator had certainly called out 'Bombs away'. I suppose in the excitement and stress during the few minutes we had been coned and shot at, we all forgot the proper drill while regaining height again after diving so low, including the 'master switch' to make the bombs live and free the circuit. But it was my responsibility to ensure that procedures were followed even under duress, and I had forgotten too. Also while milling around aimlessly over the North Sea, I should have checked with the navigator and wireless operator to sort out what was going on, either sending the second pilot back, or going back myself. But I had no inkling that the navigator had folded up, nor did the wireless operator report that he was giving good fixes to him. I felt deflated and angry with myself, and vowed that such a thing would never happen again.

Bad weather, as well as a spell of extra training with my crew, now prevented my operating for another month, but then another three good sorties within a week restored my confidence and self-esteem.

One of the interesting aspects of operational flying was the effort made by the Air Ministry to give every possible assistance to aircrew who tried to avoid capture on baling out over enemy territory. Almost the first thing that happened on my arrival at Leeming was that I had to send my tunic to the camp tailor to have silk maps sewn into the lining of each shoulder. They were of course very small scale, but expected to be of some use if the holder was trying to 'walk home' after baling out over the other side. At briefing before each operation we were given a small sealed pouch containing German marks, Dutch guilders, or French francs depending on the target. A magnetised flybutton was also part of the equipment which was highly amusing to all. This had a tiny white dot which signified the north point of the compass, and one only had to take the button off, suspend it from a piece of cotton, and a very good idea of one's direction of travel could be obtained.

When battle-dress came in and was first issued to operational aircrew – it was more comfortable than normal uniform tunics under all that flying clothing – the silk maps could not be carried since there was no lining to the battle-dress blouse, so those who smoked pipes were issued with a cheap tobacco pouch with ricepaper maps in the lining, plus a large pipe which had a small magnet hidden in the stem. As I normally smoked a pipe in those days, it soon took on a well-used look.

I almost wished that I would get the opportunity to use all this kit, as my Boy Scout mentality was rather taken with the idea of creeping around the enemy countryside, living off raw turnips and dodging enemy patrols etc., but luckily I was never called upon to demonstrate any field-craft of this nature. But we were all glad to have these aids to evasion which did at least give crews a sporting chance under certain conditions. And a good many did try; although most were picked up within hours, some kept going for days, while the occasional longer spell of freedom did occur too. Only very, very few actually evaded to safety though, without ever being captured at all, particularly after the fall of France when it became that much more difficult until the escape lines were set up at a later date.

In November I went to Duisburg, Stuttgart and Hagen in quick succession, all of them reasonably uneventful trips. After returning from Duisburg, where we had bombed the large inland docks complex in clear weather with the target easily distinguishable, we got back to our beacon at Leeming in good order, were given a green signal by Aldis lamp from the first flare, having spoken to the Flying Control Officer, and landed normally only to find that the flare-path was unusually short. I couldn't quite understand this until my landing run put me very close to a low hedge on the other side of which I could see a road, and which I then recognised as being the A1, or Great North Road as it was then. I had landed at Catterick aerodrome, the home of a fighter squadron, and only a few miles north of Leeming. They very rarely had a flare-path out, but got me down on theirs that night. I simply taxied back to the first flare and took off again for Leeming where I landed a few moments later.

At Stuttgart two nights later there was much haze over the town and we could not pick out our target, so bombed an aerodrome on the north-west of the town, returning unmolested during the long drag back. To Hagen a few nights afterwards, and this time an unusual thick mist reached from the ground to several thousand feet. We were flying above it all at 14,000ft, and saw absolutely nothing, so went down to 4,000ft to try and get below the stuff. However the diffused light from some searchlights showed that the murk probably went right down to the deck, so we loosed our load off at the searchlights since they had now been joined by some gunners who were pooping off at us blindly through the haze.

The very next night, 14 November 1940, the Luftwaffe carried out a very heavy attack on our city of Coventry with 500 bombers, which was quite obviously deliberately aimed at the civilian population. Much loss of life and great destruction of property resulted, creating the expression then in vogue, of 'being Coventrated'. This was reputed to be a reprisal ordered by Hitler for quite a minor raid which Bomber Command had made on Munich, the birthplace of Nazism, but it brought in return the most violent attacks yet made by our bombers. The target chosen was Mannheim which was raided on three consecutive nights with all we had – some 130 aircraft each night. We did not have the advantage of a radio beam for our bombing as the enemy had, so the damage was less concentrated and not so severe.

Hitler did not take the hint, however, or thought his Luftwaffe could do better, so they proceeded to demolish the centres of Southampton, Plymouth, Bristol, Liverpool, Hull, Belfast and others in quick succession, plus a full scale attack on the City of London on 29 December 1940. Although London had received almost nightly small scale raids since September, this was by far the worst.

Thus the deliberate war on civilians, demonstrated by the Luftwaffe so mercilessly on Guernica, Warsaw, Rotterdam and now on England, just begged for retaliation at last from the only nation able to administer it, and from the only military force able to carry it out, namely Bomber Command. And the whole nation yearned for it. Demanded it. And in spite of all this, we have had a host of post-war amateur historians of military matters, pontificating endlessly and drearily about the morality of the decisions made by our military and political leaders at that time and for the remainder of the war. Young men who were either not born during the war or who were still wet behind the ears at the time, have had the temerity to moralise about and criticise, decisions and events they have only read of. Having absolutely no conception of the attitudes and feelings of the population in those dark days, they still have the arrogance to criticise Bomber Command and its leaders for the policy of area bombing which began in 1941. They even have the advantage of hindsight when the unimaginable horrors of Belsen, Buchenwald, Auschwitz, Majdanek and other concentration/extermination camps have been incontrovertibly proved, plus the horrors of Lidice, Oradour, and many similar instances in Poland and Russia when whole village populations were herded into barns or churches and then destroyed by fire.

With all these undisputed facts available to them, our latter day moralists and so called 'liberalists', can still not understand that we were in a life-and-death struggle for our very existence against a ferocious and implacable enemy who would stop at nothing to gain its ends, and who had planned further unspeakable degradations against the British population – men and women – when it had conquered us too. And yet they continue to bleat on from their high-minded ivory towers, having been saved from extinction or slavery by those very people they have the impertinence to denigrate. Ye Gods! But back in 1940 the British people with one voice, and a lot more sense, called for nothing less than revenge and the complete obliteration of the scourge, by every possible means. All of us in the Command when on leave, used to be urged to 'Drop one for me' – 'Write my name on one next time' – 'Give the bastards Hell' etc., leaving us in no doubt as to the mood of the country in those days.

In December I took part in two of the raids on Mannheim, and this was really the first time that the Command tried to concentrate our forces *en-route* and over the target, all squadrons being given the same route with a time-spread on target of over two hours. This was then considered to be the minimum time in which some 130 bombers could be directed over the target airspace in order to reduce the collision factor to reasonable limits. It had not been done before, being considered to be highly dangerous, and no one knew anything about the possibilities, but only that the probabilities of collision would be too great. Little could we know that two years later some 700-800 aircraft could be put through a target area in only twenty minutes or so.

The attacks appeared to be reasonably successful too, with many fires burning as the last bombers left the town behind them. Another policy which was first tried out in these attacks, was to take many more incendiaries with us that night than we had done previously, to mix with high explosive bombs and hopefully to create more damage than just by the blast alone. How right it was. And no doubt that this decision had been arrived at because of the Luftwaffe attacks on Britain in which huge numbers of incendiaries had been used with devastating effect. Both these attacks had involved long flights of over nine hours' duration, and were reasonably uneventful if I remember correctly.

A third long haul was laid on a few days later with another attack on Berlin, which again was a mass concentration. This was my second visit to the Big City, and my thirteenth operation, so there was the usual wry comment and predictions of doom offered gratuitously by the other crews, as this was considered to be potentially dodgy always – like flying on ops on Friday the 13th.

All aircrew tended to be highly superstitious, and many had mascots, good-luck charms, rabbits' feet, special scarves given by girlfriends and so on. I once walked over half a mile to my hut and back again to the flights because while dressing into flying kit I found I had forgotten a bent ha'penny which I always carried. By the end of the war it had become brightly polished and much thinner through being permanently in my pocket. Others would have very deliberate set patterns in the way they prepared for operations, always exactly the same. One bomb aimer we had at one squadron used to pee against the starboard wheel before climbing into his aircraft, this being his personal propitiation to the gods, devils, gremlins, or whoever it was that controlled his destiny and had to be placated first. It was always a bit of a joke really, though indulging one's personal whim was taken very seriously.

Anyway, this didn't turn out to be an unlucky 13th for us, as we had a comparatively trouble-free ride. No 4 Group was on first to try and start up fires for 3 and 5 Groups, which seemed to be fairly successful. We ourselves chose to make our bombing run in a sort of stretched glide at a quarter throttle, going down from 14,000ft to attack from 9,000ft, as at this time it was considered to be a useful ploy for putting off the sound locators which could not pick us up if we were throttled well back. At least this was the theory, and we would try out anything in those days, although I didn't think enough of it to use it again, as one lost too much valuable height in the process, and we were already being pushed higher by the increased efficiency and accuracy of the enemy flak and searchlight defences. Incidentally, our route that night had been right across the North Sea towards Denmark and into the Baltic, turning down south-east after that on a straight run to Berlin, and avoiding the heavily defended zones now stretching almost solidly from Hamburg to Cologne.

Our last sortie for 1940 was on 29 December when an attack on Frankfurt was ordered, and which produced for me the worst experience of icing I had yet encountered, or ever met again in fact. We all flew through moderate icing occasionally, particularly if a tour of operations coincided with winter months, but apart from the cases mentioned earlier, this normally took the form of a sort of hoar frost appearing on the leading edges of the wings and on the front of the cockpit canopy and front turret. It forced the pilot to fly on instruments, but was usually thrown off by the pulsating membranes along the wings and did not collect on the airscrews. All of it would come off when the aircraft came out of the cloud causing it.

But this was something different. The night was very dark at take-off with a lot of high cloud, and on leaving the Suffolk coast at about 3,000ft and starting to climb for the Dutch coast, we ran into a gentle misty drizzle – which had not been forecast, needless to add – and were soon engulfed in thin wet cloud. It was very cold, and the drizzle froze into ice the moment it touched the aeroplane, giving a coating of crystal-clear glazing on the front of the wings and cockpit. We had switched on the pulsators from the first, but as we climbed higher pure ice was piling up on the leading edges and spreading slowly backwards down the wings, the de-icers becoming completely over loaded and useless. Forcing a side window open, we could see it all from the glare of the exhausts of our Merlin engines. We struggled to 8,000ft hoping to clear the cloud and wet, but could get no higher owing to the weight of the ice and more importantly because the deposit had altered the shape of the wing aerofoil section and therefore the flying characteristics.

The aircraft was as soggy as a wet brick and becoming difficult to handle, and great chunks of ice were being thrown off the airscrews and thumping ominously against the sides. It was time I tried to get down to warmer air, so I put the nose down and dived gently to escape, noticing immediately that there was no increase in the airspeed. This could only mean one thing, which was that the 'pitot' head itself had been gummed up with ice and a large blob had formed on that too in spite of the heater element in the nose of the tube to overcome this very problem.

So now I could only guess at our airspeed by keeping the rev counters and boost gauges at normal, and by the feel of the aeroplane, all of which was somewhat difficult with the heavy coating of ice gumming everything up. We got down to 1,000ft – still on course and probably over Holland by then – and with the amount of ice we were carrying slowly increasing and creating great difficulty in the handling of the controls, I regretfully decided that we must turn for home, making a wide careful turn on to the necessary course. The ice started to come off at 500ft, with much banging and cracking. The navigator had coded up a signal to Group and we got back home after more than five hours of instrument flying under tiring and somewhat nerve-racking circumstances.

There had not been many aircraft out that night, and a number of others had suffered as we did, although all had experienced difficulty of some sort it had not been as bad for some who had missed the worst quite by chance.

During the autumn of 1940 it was becoming obvious from photographic reconnaissance that our bombers were not finding their targets as often as they should, and that bombs were being dropped all too frequently miles away from where they should have been deposited, and the reasons for which have already been explained. The crews had conscientiously been doing their best but it was worrying us who had the job to do as well as those in higher places.

At Leeming under our fiery Station Commander 'Kong' Staton, and our thoughtful Squadron Commander Sidney Bufton, we had even then been trying out various means of improving our accuracy, and therefore results, by using experienced crews to try and lead the way as it were. One was to give incendiaries to only the best crews to try and show the way to the target, and prevent the newer boys from starting false fires in the wrong places. I well remember an occasion over Lorient when I was detailed to shoot off a certain combination of coloured Very cartridges when – and if – we had definitely identified the target.

I was also to call up the rest of the squadron on R/T to tell them to watch for the signal if it was being fired off. In fact we did see the docks and pooped off the necessary colours, calling all 'Rabit' aircraft as I did so. (This was the squadron call sign at the time but I never quite understood why only one b!) It didn't appear to be very successful since nobody answered me, so God knows where they had all got to. But it does show that we were very conscious of the problem at operational level, and not at all complacent but trying to do something about it quite early on. One of the Mannheim raids just mentioned was started off by experienced crews in Wellingtons of 3 Group with the same objective, dropping nothing but incendiaries in the first stage of the attack. These then, were the first tentative experiments towards finding a target marking system to improve the bomber capability.

It is interesting to note therefore, and my great pleasure to give the credit where it is really due, that when Sidney Bufton was posted in April 1941 at the end of his tour of operations, it was to the Directorate of Bombing Operations at Air Ministry as Group Captain Deputy Director. His chief, the Director, was Air Vice-Marshal Ivelaw Chapman who had also recently served in 4 Group as a Station Commander. It was those two between them who started the long haul to get a specially trained and equipped force for the specific task of target marking. From April 1941 the struggle to find more sophisticated equipment and navigational aids had therefore begun, so that a specialist force would be equipped with the most modern scientific aids possible. It was an even greater struggle to get the policy accepted, the Commander-in-Chief himself being the greatest hurdle to surmount as he was sincerely opposed to the concept. However, he was eventually over-ruled by the Air Council, and the Pathfinder Force was created over a year later in July 1942. It became famous under its commander Air Vice-Marshal Don Bennett who has been credited with the idea, but who in fact was simply given command of the force from its inception, although he may have had some influence at a late stage in it being finally accepted. But it was Chapman and Bufton who originated the whole idea and did all the spade work to get it adopted against much opposition.

This is not to detract from the contribution to the success of the project once it was formed which 'The Don' made from then on. He was the ideal choice for the post of Commander – insisted upon by Air Marshal Harris against more opposition, because once he was ordered to create this force he saw Bennett as the only leader of it he would countenance. Bennett was fifteen or twenty years younger than any of the other Group Commanders, some of whom showed considerable jealousy at the appointment. But Don was undoubtedly the most efficient pilot, navigator, and general expert on all flying equipment and theory, ever produced by any air force. His drive and expertise made the Pathfinder Force the great success it became and which made a tremendous impact on the eventual achievements of the Command as a whole.

There was one Whitley pilot who had made quite a name

for himself in those early days by inventing his own personal method of getting down in fog when he was lost in conditions of nil visibility at night. His system was to trim the aircraft 'tail heavy', then to keep going as slowly as possible with flaps half lowered but with plenty of throttle to keep from stalling, so that his aeroplane would now be sinking steadily in a nose-up attitude rather like a lift, but with a forward speed as well of about 80mph, all of which a Whitley would perform. The crew would then strap themselves in at their crash positions and wait patiently for their arrival on the deck with undercart retracted, hopefully to slither to a juddering halt without undue damage!

The wretched crew must have accepted this with some trepidation, although it was probably better than baling out if they thought that they might be over the sea; but the pilot was extremely confident although it was a very dodgy way of going about it. Fantastically enough, it worked twice. The first time they landed somewhere in Lincolnshire, where as everybody knows there are few hills and almost no trees, and they all stepped out unharmed. On the second occasion they landed in the sea although they had believed themselves to be over terra firma. They all got happily into their rubber dinghy having made a perfect ditching, when they realised that the aircraft was apparently floating well and attributed this phenomenon to the practically empty petrol tanks. So they tied up alongside as it were, but ready to cast off quickly should the aeroplane decide to go under at any moment. But as dawn approached, they began to hear strange noises apparently coming from each side of them, and as the fog slowly lifted they discovered that land lay on two sides, and not very far distant either. They had 'arrived' in the Humber estuary, up-stream, with the aircraft firmly settled on a mud-bank in the middle.

So our cheerful optimist was then called for an interview with his CO who had to explain to him that so far on these two occasions he had been blessed with the luck of a pox doctor's clerk, which could under no circumstances be expected to last. Also that there were certain other officially recommended procedures which he should adopt in future if he wished to stay alive, rather than to subject himself and his whole crew to the risks of flying smack into a hill, barn, wood, house, electric power lines, or other equally nasty obstacle with which the English landscape is cluttered to the detriment of lost aviators. And he – the CO – did not want a crew risked in this manner to be written off in one grand prang, thank you very much.

The Whitley was a sturdy aeroplane with few vices, if any. It could take a lot of punishment, and was a pleasure to fly if a trifle on the slow side, but well liked by those who had to fly them on operations. There was a marked tendency to swing to port on take-off because of the engine torque created by the two 1,000hp Rolls Royce Merlin engines which powered it. But swing was experienced to some degree in most aircraft, and easy to counter by coarse use of the rudder, or by opening the port throttle in advance of the starboard one in the early stages of the take-off run.

One late afternoon, however, we had a take-off in conditions of mist and poor visibility which was expected to clear during the night, but it was considered to be safe enough for take-off if a flare-path were laid to give a suitable guideline in the mist. I was in the control tower, not being on the crew list for that night. We could not see the flares at all because of the mist, but heard several aircraft take off and climb away satisfactorily. They would have been out of it in seconds once off the ground, as it was not deep.

Suddenly, however, we heard the roar of Merlins at full throttle which seemed to be rapidly approaching, and a Whitley suddenly loomed out of the mist, its wheels just clear of the ground and going like the clappers heading straight for the Control Tower. We all threw ourselves flat on the floor as we envisaged the roof being swiped off, but the pilot just managed to yank the nose up enough to clear us by inches, it seemed. Rather a dicey moment, and I'll wager that the pilot was having kittens himself when he saw the hangars and flying control appearing out of the murk at him about 150 yards away when his aircraft had only just come unstuck on take-off. He had obviously lost the flares on the initial swing but ploughed on thinking he could keep the aeroplane straight without any datum line to go on. How wrong he was, and so nearly ended in disaster. One Whitley, fully laden with bombs and petrol, flying full tilt into a hangar and taking the flying control building with it, doesn't bear thinking about. Yet the possibility of such incidents was never very far away in those days, and the wonder is that they did not occur more frequently, when safety standards had to be subordinated so often to operational necessity.

Fog on the ground was another nightmare for crews then, as there were not the aids to prevent it from being a deadly enemy. Many crews were killed in training and on returning from operations, when fog unexpectedly caught them still in the air and they attempted to land in order to save their aircraft, rather than bale out and let the aeroplane crash somewhere.

One night I was detailed to take a party of men out to lay a flare-path on the top of Sutton Bank about 1,000ft up in the North Yorkshire moors to the east of Thirsk. Fog was expected to form in the Vale of York, where all our aerodromes were situated, by the time our aircraft were due back from the night's operation. So we set up a long flare-path in the heather and sat back in a lorry waiting patiently for the expected twenty or thirty aeroplanes to turn up. We could see the fog thickening up down below us in the valley, but in the end only one Whitley arrived, much to our disappointment as all the others had managed to creep in somewhere, even if not at their own stations.

The Group was not so lucky on another night when fog unexpectedly clamped down in the Yorkshire area as well as all over the country with only a few clear areas. Three of our crews had to bale out having insufficient petrol to divert to a clear aerodrome further south, while two others managed to land safely in other counties. No 4 Group lost no fewer than eight aircraft that night over England, although happily all the crews were safe, having baled out all over the countryside successfully. Command lost more aircraft over England than over Germany on that operation.

The responsibility for making the final decision to send out his bomber forces on any given night in bad weather conditions for the return, must have been an awesome weight on the shoulders of the C-in-C. Continual telephone conferences on the 'scrambler' phones between the various Group Commanders and Command HQ with the senior Met officer on tap, would be called right up to take-off time on occasions. And these decisions could not be, and were not, taken lightly. Sometimes we had even got into our aircraft and started up the engines before a cancellation came through, which was highly frustrating to the crews and more than wearing on the nerves. Having got keyed-up and ready to go, it was galling to suddenly 'let go' as it were, knowing that tomorrow you would have to go through the whole process again anyway.

Things improved dramatically when the FIDO airstrips were completed and in operation late in 1943. These were strung out along the east coast from Manston in Kent, Woodbridge in Suffolk, Bridlington in Yorkshire, and at Blackbushe in Surrey as well. The 'Fog Identification and Dispersal Operation' was the official term, I think, and they were laid in one direction only, there being no wind in foggy weather. But they were extra long, and three runways wide, so that large numbers of aircraft could be got down very quickly if necessary. Also if one runway was closed because of a crashed aeroplane cluttering up the landing strip, there would still be two more available for incoming bombers still needing to be got down. In fact they were designed to receive our whole bomber force if ever it became necessary.

To enable pilots to see the runways through the thickest

fog, the whole landing area was surrounded by pipe-lines through which petrol was circulated. Specially designed jets were ignited to create a great rectangle of flames, the sheer heat from it all being enough to clear the fog from the immediate locality and allow our aircraft to get down in safety under conditions which would otherwise have caused tremendous losses over this country. This enabled the C-in-C to order offensive operations on nights when otherwise there would have been no flying.

In practice, once they had become established, they became invaluable for the reception of bombers which had received extensive damage from enemy action and needed extra long runways and good lighting because flying controls had been shot away or wheels would not come down etc. They also enabled our Mosquito bomber force to keep up a relentless attack on Berlin at one stage, of over eighty nights running during very bad weather, because we had a safe haven for their return, even in the very worst of weather. Moreover, just as important as this, it gave a tremendous amount of confidence to all our crews knowing full well that they could get down somewhere safely even if the worst possible weather had overtaken our bases while they were away over Germany. They were an outstanding success, and saved very many crews and aircraft which would otherwise have been lost.

To return to 1940, on New Year's Eve it snowed practically all night and started three months of very cold and wet weather which slowed down the tempo of operations as far as we were concerned, as the aerodrome became very soft and quite unusable at times. The whole perimeter round which the aircraft were parked began to get churned up by the constant traffic of vans and lorries needed for the servicing and maintenance. Aircraft frequently got bogged down to the wheel axles when being fuelled or bombed up, or even while taxiing if they hit a soft spot. We had to have a heavy duty caterpillar tractor standing by at all times to rescue bogged down aeroplanes, and it was in constant use. It was hopeless without tarmac perimeter tracks, hard standings or runways, and when the ground was not actually frozen we had to fly off unloaded to other aerodromes in the Group where their soil conditions were much better than ours, for fuel and bombs to be put on so that we could operate away from our own station, when required. It made life very difficult and our ground crews worked wonders to keep the aircraft serviceable.

Of course, it had been realised earlier that all flying could grind to a halt in really wet weather, and all new airfields under construction by now were getting the full requirement of concrete runways, taxi tracks, and aircraft dispersal points. A crash programme of adding these necessities to all existing airfields was put in hand from the spring of 1941 onwards so that all airfields were 'weather proof' by the winter of 1942.

So I only managed to clock up half-a-dozen trips in those three dreary months although the squadron operated more than that of course, and we were briefed for a good many more which were cancelled before we could get into the air because of bad weather over England. This slowing down of the rate of operations was an awful bind to the crews generally, because everyone wanted to get on with their tours once they were in a squadron, to complete the obligatory thirty operations as quickly as possible.

Hanging about because of bad weather was most unpopular, particularly when briefing had been given, or even worse having dressed into flying kit before the 'ops scrubbed' call came through, knowing that the whole performance would probably be repeated the next day.

In January we had an attack ordered on the docks at Brest, where one of the German 'Hipper' Class cruisers had taken refuge – believed damaged – and the Command was instructed to try and keep it there. I was taking a completely new crew on their first trip, and it became quite a memorable one for me – almost amusing in a sort of way. The weather was absolutely clear but dark, although the coastline of the

Brest Peninsula was easy to pick out. Making our run directly from north to south as we approached from the Channel, all our armour-piercing bombs were to be dropped in one stick from 14,000ft.

There was a fair amount of searchlight and flak activity as we approached, which was to be expected with the presence of a capital ship in a port so close to Britain. But we were not singled out for special attention and simply had to plough through the box barrage which was being thrown up over the target. This was normal defence procedure, and always looked rather nasty from a distance, but did not seem so bad once you were in it unless you were unlucky enough to be in the way of a shell happening to come a bit too close. Shrapnel hits were common, but a vital direct hit most unlucky in barrages of that nature.

But no welcoming 'Bombs Gone' cry came up from the navigator, who soon told me that he had not been able to see the target and would I 'go round again please?' I made a mental note that I had got a responsible chap here who was obviously not going to chuck his bombs down any old where just to get rid of them quickly, and was happy to oblige him to encourage him for the future in this very admirable attitude towards his job. So I circled round and went through the defences again. I wasn't at all worried about the danger of collision, because with the comparatively few aircraft over a target at any given moment in those days this was not the serious risk it became later when so many bombers had to be concentrated in such a short time, and 'going round again' became too dicey to contemplate with so many aeroplanes in a small piece of sky.

Sergeant Ottway was giving me steady and unruffled steering instructions over the intercom, and I again thought how reliable he would be, and a good influence on the rest of the crew who were all NCO's. But again the expected 'Bombs Gone' did not materialise and I was asked to 'go round again'. I wondered somewhat wryly if he thought we were on a practice bombing detail over the Otmoor ranges, and turned round for another run, having another good look at the coastline to see if there had been any change in visibility. But it was still absolutely clear down below, and when he took us through the target for the third time without dropping the bombs I clearly had to take the matter in hand.

Circling the area for our fourth run I tipped the aircraft in a steep bank and looked down the port wing at the target area myself. The other members of the crew had been absolutely quiet all this time and I could sense the edginess creeping in. The second pilot had already given me a quizzical sort of look which I had answered with a grin, hoping that it didn't look too sickly! But what I saw on the ground of course, through the open window at my side, explained everything. The coastlines were perfectly visible, but the docks and a large part of Brest were covered by plumes of smoke emanating from a long line of smoke generators sited up-wind of the dock area and therefore hiding our prey. Three dummy runs over that hot spot were quite enough, so I told Ottway that the only thing he could do in those circumstances was to take a line from a promontory or bay he could identify, to the estimated target point on his map where the great ship was berthed, and let the bombs go on that part of the smoke to his best calculations.

The barrage had intensified during all this time, and the searchlights seemed to be getting closer and more organised. I suppose we were more or less on our own by this time too, but thankfully we broke through once again unscathed at the other side of the target area, and turned north after diving slightly to increase our lumbering speed away from the defences.

After we left the French coast behind I ordered the coffee to be broached and the tension eased. A voice came over the intercom: 'If you want to do that sort of thing regularly, Bill, don't ask me to come with you' and another one added immediately, 'Nor any of us either'. They were light-hearted quips which were not really seriously intended, but which nevertheless summed up the anxious moments so recently experienced. I told Ottway to take no notice. He had done his job in a most responsible manner in not wanting to lob his bombs down on the unfortunate French population if he could possibly avoid it. But he had expected that he would be able to see the ship – or at 'least the docks, and the smokescreen had quite upset his ideas of how things would look.

Another attack on Boulogne docks in February to baptise another new crew was laid on for me, and the defence obliged by peppering us with a few minor holes. There was fog all over Yorkshire on our return and we couldn't get down on any 4 Group flare-path, having to retrace our course back to Lincolnshire which was still quite clear, and where we landed quite easily without any difficulty.

On another occasion around this time we were returning from a sortie and on course to Yorkshire from Orfordness which was one of our regular landfall points. The whole country seemed clear, but very dark as there was some high cloud obliterating the stars. But cruising up through Norfolk and Lincolnshire all the bomber station beacons were flashing their welcome signals with several flare-paths lit, always a great comfort on the few occasions it happened like that, and we were dead on track at 2,000ft as we crossed the Humber. But then a huge black wall of solid cloud confronted us as we were obviously about to enter a dirty great 'front' which had not been forecast. Sure enough the cloud and rain forced us down to 600ft, at which height we plodded on northwards seeing absolutely nothing until we arrived at the Leeming beacon which luckily we hit spot on as the visibility was very poor. There was no flare-path alight, so we had to circle the beacon while it was being lit by a surprised and sleepy flare party.

A 'BFX' (diversion signal) had been sent out to all 4 Group aircraft that night because of this front unexpectedly coming down country from the north-west. For some reason or other – the usual wireless set trouble I expect – we had not received this signal telling us to land in Lincolnshire, and we were the only aircraft to return to Yorkshire that night. I went in to land as soon as the flares were ready, but unfortunately while speaking to control over the R/T had forgotten to ask for the barometric pressure at ground level so that I could re-set my altimeter. This was all part of the drill on arrival back at base as the barometric pressure nearly always altered during the time we were away on a long flight.

Flying control had not volunteered the information either, and as I finally approached the first flare, about 400 yards in front of me, a mass of dark trees suddenly reared ahead between us and the flare-path, and seeming to be almost above us. A long burst of full throttle enabled us to scrape in and plonk down at the first flare safe but a little shaken. I had been unable to see anything of the ground in the darkness and rain. My altimeter still showed 200ft on the dial when we were on the deck, so we had been gaily stooging up Yorkshire at just under 400ft to keep under the cloud base in the rain and pitch dark. Seeing absolutely nothing of the ground below we had not realised it had been so close. Our gremlins were being friendly that night.

Sometimes when one had been flying for any length of time high up on a very dark night, and even with stars visible, one got the sensation that you were not flying level at all, but in some other attitude you could not describe. Even the stars seemed to be underneath you and with no horizon to judge by it seemed that you were flying into nothingness. Your instruments would tell you that everything was all right but your 'feel' had gone somehow. You then had to discard your senses and stick to your trusty instruments, cutting in George if necessary while you regained your equilibrium. I don't know if other pilots ever had this odd sensation, but I certainly did on two or three occasions only.

At other times on lovely clear nights and almost blue-black heavens filled with bright stars really shining, everything would seem unnaturally peaceful. On one of those very few such occasions – probably during the summer or early autumn 1941 – I saw no fewer than eight shooting stars sweep across the sky in huge arcs over a period of little more than an hour. From 15,000ft up, they started low down on the horizon to describe a complete half circle before disappearing again on the opposite side of the world, the whole trajectory taking several seconds to complete. I am normally a bit of a Philistine and not much given to artistic or philosophical musings but it was impossible not to wonder then at the sheer mind-bending immensity of the universe and of space, leading on into infinity and never ending anywhere. Until, that is, the navigator suddenly asked if you could see the English coast ahead, or a searchlight sprang up from nowhere to jolt you out of reverie into reality.

Another visually dramatic experience occurred one night over Holland on our way home from a German target. We had climbed to about 16,000ft to get above a 'frontal system' which had loomed ahead with a mass of giant cumulo nimbus clouds towering in parts well above us. We had to fly round these to avoid the turbulent and ice-laden interiors we would undoubtedly have encountered if we had tried to fly straight through them. Suddenly the clouds below became illuminated with brilliant flashes of light and, naturally assuming that we were being shot at, I automatically started to take violent evasive action. However I realised quickly that this was not so because of the dazzling whiteness of the light, and the way it filled the clouds below us.

It was, of course, lightning which was flickering in the clouds, enabling us to see as if in daylight right into the deep valleys from the peaks we were skirting or skimming. And this continued for about twenty minutes, and the unusual thing about it was that for the whole period it was not just a case of the occasional or even frequent flash, but a continual intermittent flicker, the like of which I have never seen from the ground nor ever again in the air.

These moments were unrepeatable even if nature itself

had obliged with an encore, because later on our bomber force went out always several hundred strong and bunched together for safety, and we had to keep urgent and permanent watch against the possibility of collision from friends or for enemy night fighters prowling the bomber stream for their victims. We had no time then to examine the beauties of nature, or ponder on the mysteries of the universe.

During the first two winters of the war when constant bad weather added to the difficulties of our bombers, 'letting down' through cloud on return to base was sometimes a bit unnerving in conditions of 7 to 10/10ths cover, if a wireless fix had not been obtained when nearing home. Between York and Northallerton where all 4 Group stations were sited at that time, we had the north York moors to the east, and particularly near to Leeming and Dishforth, while the Yorkshire dales lay off to the west. So with the hills at 1,200 to 1,500ft five miles on our east side, and others at 1,800 to 2,400ft on the west side only twelve miles distant, descending simply on R/T contact was a chancy business.

R/T range was about 15 miles we were told, and one night, with about 8/10ths cloud cover all over the country and frequent snow showers in Yorkshire, we had arrived over our base on dead reckoning only having last seen the ground and got a pin-point visual fix when crossing the Dutch coast on the way back. I called up flying control over the R/T on ETA and was delightfully surprised when they answered me first time. However, my pleasure was somewhat dimmed when they informed us that the cloud base was only 1,300ft as we were flying through the tops at 7,000ft and had to get down to break cloud.

We could see nothing of the ground of course, and no beacons either because of the cloud but I throttled back and gingerly lost height, collecting a little white ice on the way down and flying on a north bearing hoping to be over the valley – preferably in the middle! It was a horrid feeling as we got to 1,500ft with still a couple of hundred more to go before we broke cloud. If we happened to be only 10 miles out to either side we might have just a few feet to spare with luck, or fly smack into a hill if otherwise. We were all holding our breath as the cloud thinned and we broke free into reasonable visibility with no snow shower in the vicinity. The rear gunner spotted a beacon from which we soon found our own. At that moment I could not help envying the squadrons operating from East Anglia where there were no hills to worry about. Some losses were caused by our proximity to those hills in 4 Group, but happily rather fewer than might have been expected. The nagging worry was always there in those early days though under certain weather conditions, but it disappeared later when improved navigational aids and much more reliable radios came into use.

It was during 1941 that we had a little extra fun with two items we took with us occasionally. The first were code-named 'Razzles' for some unknown reason, and were simply two small pieces of celluloid about 4in square with a square of phosphorus sandwiched in between. These had to be dropped out through the flare chute when over Germany on the way to, or return from, a target. Stored immersed in water in special containers, they ignited on contact with the air after drying off, and were supposed to start up forest fires, set crops and barns alight or even houses if lucky, and generally cause a nuisance to the enemy wherever we had passed by aloft. I don't think that they were all that successful and were discontinued after a few months, but they gave us a bit of fun while they lasted.

They had one unfriendly side-effect though. They frequently got caught up in the aircraft tail units after they had been snatched by the slipstream on emerging from the flare chutes. And although the 130mph blast would prevent them from igniting in the air, after we had landed and were taxiing thankfully back to a dispersal point on the perimeter of the airfield, a small bonfire would suddenly break out at the tail end and a minor panic would ensue in order to prevent any serious damage from being perpetrated on the rest of the aeroplane by this, our own offensive weapon. Perhaps this is why they were stopped as they probably did more damage to us than to the enemy!

The other amusing diversion we were given at that time was to throw out small canvas bags of tea over Holland. The Dutch were having a dreadful time so apart from dropping leaflets to them which we did frequently to give them all the latest news, some boffin thought up this idea as a psychological morale booster for them as well. So we slung these little sacks down the flare chutes with gay abandon. They each had a large label attached with a message of cheer from the RAF and we thoroughly enjoyed doing it.

I know for certain that it was a gesture much appreciated by the recipients because of an amusing sequel many years later, when my wife and I were dining in a small bistro in St Tropez. I was wearing an RAF blazer, and a chap sitting next to me in the crowded little room suddenly turned to me and said, 'I think you must have been in the Royal Air Force?' I admitted my guilt, and we got chatting. He was a Dutchman and spoke perfect English, was very pro-British and even more pro-RAF.

I asked him if he had ever known anyone who had found any of the tea bags we had dropped over Holland in 1941 and he nearly went mad with delight. He most certainly had, himself and many others, and he then stood up and announced to all and sundry that here was a chap who had actually dropped sacks of tea over Holland on his way to bomb Germany etc. etc. We were somewhat embarrassed by his public display of enthusiasm which seemed to me to fall a bit flat at some tables, so I expect that there were a few Germans in the audience! Nevertheless I pulled him down on to his seat and our own version of an Anglo-Dutch entente cordiale rapidly developed into a very pleasant evening.

Our crews in 10 Squadron used to amuse themselves too by throwing out empty bottles and other objects they thought might annoy the recipients when over German territory. It was popularly believed that empty bottles made a whistling noise as they descended but whether this was really so no one actually knew, and the practice continued for quite a while. One humourist once inserted a boxer's gum shield into a set of false teeth, wrapped it up in a large cardboard box tied with coloured ribbon, and addressed it to 'Adolf Hitler – Berlin'. This was shoved out of the lower hatch on one of the visits we paid to the Big City to the vast amusement of the perpetrator and his crew.

A more practical type invented and built a bomb of his own to lob out on one occasion. It consisted of a metal dust-bin filled with stones and rubble, in the middle of which had been buried a wad of explosive and a 40lb oil bomb which had been scrounged from a chum in the armoury. An impact fuse ensured that the whole thing would go off with a bang on hitting the deck. The lid was wired on, and the contraption duly expelled from the side door of a Whitley while over a German target. All a bit childish, it might be thought, but quite amusing to us all at the time, as well as bringing a little light relief to the sterner realities which otherwise engaged our attention. And a good all-round morale booster as well, in a funny sort of way.

In March and April 1941, with the weather improving and the surface of the grass airfield returning to a more or less solid state once more, the operational tempo increased and I logged up four or five more sorties including two on 8th and 9th April – Kiel and Berlin. This was my third visit to Berlin and we were once again to use the long route which was then favoured for this target. This was to go straight out across the North Sea to Denmark, and cross Schleswig Holstein between Kiel and Hamburg, then to turn down to Berlin on a south-easterly course. This way we spent much less time over German soil, had a long trouble-free stooge across the North Sea both ways, and avoided having to fly twice through the wide, heavy, searchlight and flak defence zones in Western

Germany and Holland. The crews all liked this route even though it meant spending ten hours or more in the air.

It was a clear night, and we got a good ground pin-point position at the Baltic coast on the way in. There was not a lot of activity as we approached the target area, other than a few odd searchlights probing the skies in the usual slow and deliberate manner. As we made a wide circle carefully searching the ground for the target, there was a sudden almighty 'crump' dead ahead about 25 yards in front of us, and almost immediately we flew through the acrid black smoke of the burst. Strangely I had seen no flash, and we received no more direct personal attention although that had been a damned good shot and the defences were now thoroughly stirred and highly active, with many searchlights swinging round the sky.

My navigator, Sergeant Butler, now took me over the target and let our load go whereupon I turned on a northerly course to get ready for the run back to the Baltic. The rear gunner reported only one fire burning which must have been from our attack, as we had carried a high proportion of incendiaries. As we drew further away, the gunner was waxing lyrical about the fire we had created, so I orbited to have a good look, and we all had the satisfying sight of an unusually bright white fire blazing on the ground with a long plume of pure white smoke streaming merrily away from it. We never knew what we had hit, of course, but it must surely have been something useful, and we could still see it from many miles away on the return route.

After crossing the enemy coast for the long drag back across the North Sea, I handed over to my second 'Dicky' who was a new arrival to the squadron – a Flight Lieutenant Skinner. Settling him into the pilot's seat, I turned on the fuel cock to the reserve tank which was the normal drill on very long flights, to use up the reserve and turn back to the main tanks again for the final stage. I told him that the fuel would be used up by about a certain time and to watch out for it in order to transfer back on to main tanks quickly. I then settled in my seat as comfortably as I could for a quiet snooze since it was a clear night with no undue worries expected.

After about an hour or so however, I was jolted out of my semi-consciousness most dramatically, because the comforting drone of our two Merlins suddenly and alarmingly faded away to complete quietness as the reserve petrol was finally used up. I had turned the reserve fuel cock off, and the main tanks on, in an instant split-second reaction before the pilot knew what was happening even, and the engines picked up cheerfully. But my heart was thumping madly and took a few moments to settle down while I vowed that I would never try and rest again like that no matter how peaceful and quiet the circumstances appeared to be.

It was at the start of one of these operations in March or April when we had just climbed into our aeroplane at dispersal, and still in daylight. The ground staff were fussing around outside as usual with their last minute preparations and I had my head down in the 'office' going through the pre-flight cockpit drill. Then looking up to start the engines I saw the ground crew at that very moment suddenly dive out of sight under the belly of our aircraft. Looking round puzzled, but sensing something diabolical about to erupt, I glanced upwards and saw a large and menacing Heinkel 111 droning sedately across the aerodrome at no more than 700ft on an easterly course. The front gunner was hosing down a stream of tracer from his single pop-gun, which was arriving quite harmlessly in the grass along the flare path which had already been lit. It continued straight on towards the coast without coming round again, and I cursed the fact that we had not got our engines started so that our rear gunner could have given him a squirt. Without the starboard engine running there was no power to the rear turret. It appeared that it was probably a weather recce flight which the Germans were sending out to our coasts in those days, and the keen type Luftwaffe pilot had decided to have a look at our countryside as well. He could have done us a bit of no good if he had carried a few bombs.

I had now got over twenty operations behind me and had visions of completing my tour before mid-summer with better weather and more opportunities for flying, but it was not to be. In the middle of April I was posted off to Linton-on-Ouse a little further south nearer to York, together with three or four of the most experienced crews from 10 Squadron, to be the nucleus of the two new four-engined Halifax squadrons about to be formed there. I was therefore a founder member of No 76 Squadron while Squadron Leader Willy Tait had already started with No 35 Squadron there. In fact he gave me my first dual 'circuits and bumps' on this new type, and after a little practice on my own I then gave instruction to the other pilots who were being posted in to build up the new squadron. From then on, Willy, myself, and Flight Lieutenant Lane converted all the new pilots who were sent in.

It is worth mentioning here that Willy Tait already had earned a DSO and a DFC at this time, and he later became the only man in any service who was awarded the DSO no less than four times, as well as two DFC's. It was an incredible feat culminating in the sinking of the *Tirpitz* in a Norwegian fjord when he led the famous 617 Squadron on that epic operation.

CHAPTER THREE

Four Engines

WE started working up to operational standard as more experienced pilots and crews were posted in. Squadron Leader Bickford arrived to command the second flight and eventually Wing Commander Jarman to take over the squadron. I gave them both their initial dual on the Mark I Halifax, and crew training continued until early June when we all flew up to Middleton St George near Darlington to a new station which was to be our operational base with the new heavy bombers. No 35 Squadron stayed on at Linton to operate from there.

During May, the Luftwaffe was sufficiently interested in the beginnings of our new big bomber force to mount an attack on the aerodrome at Linton one night with three or four Ju88's. In clear conditions and a full moon, they made a bit of a mess of a few buildings round the flying control area of the tarmac, but no aircraft were damaged as they were all well dispersed. Our own of 76 Squadron were safely some miles away in a large open field at Tholthorpe which later was to become one of the satellite bomber stations which were already being built to house the greatly enlarged bomber force then planned. Sadly though, there were a few casualties among the personnel caused by the vicious fragmentation bombs used, one of whom was the Station Commander, Group Captain Garroway, who had been directing the defence and fire fighting operations during the attack. He had only just arrived on the station too, having been posted to the Command a day or two before.

At Middleton St George we soon got stuck into the war again, and had been joined there by 78 Squadron still equipped with Whitleys. For about half the trips I had done with 10 Squadron I had carried a regular crew, changing only the second 'Dicky' when the need for giving operational experience to new pilots arose. So Sergeants Gretlyer (navigator), Heaton (wireless operator) and Phillips (rear gunner) had all come with me to 76 Squadron as an experienced nucleus crew on its formation.

The four-engined bombers carried a crew of seven, as against the four in twin aircraft, because an extra gunner had to be taken for a mid-upper turret which now had to be permanently manned. Also two new aircrew categories of bomb aimer and flight engineer had been created because of the increased complexity of cockpit instruments which were now in two sections. The pilot now had only those instruments absolutely necessary to the flying of the aeroplane and performance of the engines – the standard I.F. Panel, flap gauge, boost and rev counters, brake pressure gauge etc – quite enough to have to look at and constantly check during flight without having to worry about all the cocks and gauges now on the flight engineer's panel (petrol, engine temperatures, oil levels, hydraulic systems, airscrew feathering, electrical circuits, and so on).

The bomb aimer was responsible for the complete bombing system and electrical circuit, even with control of the master switch which was one more worry taken from the pilot. He also helped the navigator to work the Gee Box and H2S radar when those came into use, and which will be mentioned again later on. He was also a sort of pilot's mate, helping at take-off and landing with such things as ensuring that the throttles were properly locked, even opening up the throttles in some cases, setting the degree of 'flaps' called for by the pilot, manipulating the undercarriage lever on the orders of the pilot etc.

These modern aeroplanes were now so much more sophisticated that much more attention to detail was required to fly them. It was not that they were difficult to fly, because the Halifax was a very pleasant aircraft to handle in the air, but being so large and complicated they needed that much more careful pre-flight checking and handling at take-off or landing.

We started operating during the second week in June 1941, and I took my first Halifax I on an operation on the night of 20 June. Kiel was the target, but I nearly didn't get there because it almost ended before it had begun. Middleton St George was situated about 10 miles from the centre of Middlesborough, and this industrial town and port was protected against enemy attack with balloons besides the normal AA guns and searchlights.

Having taken off at dusk on a clear summer evening, we made a wide circle inland before I set the course given to me by our navigator. Concentrating intently on the instruments and cockpit adjustments with my head down in the 'office' to make sure that everything was in order, I had just lined up the compass to the correct heading when Butch Heaton at the wireless set suddenly called out over the intercom: 'We're heading into the balloon barrage, Skipper'. At almost the same moment I heard in my earphones the alarming high-pitched buzz of the 'squeakers' which indicated that we were indeed flying close to the balloons. This warning device was broadcast from the ground where balloons were being flown, on the same frequency as our R/T, and supposedly to warn us that we were approaching a balloon defended area. The range was very limited for obvious reasons, and in this case was so short that we were in amongst the balloons before we picked up the warning.

We were then flying at 4,000ft, and glancing upwards I saw those damned great fat balloons sitting there about 7–800ft above us, and clearly visible in the setting sun, although the ground below was in dark shadow. I couldn't see the cables of course, but the balloons themselves indicated the direction of the wind since they naturally all pointed on the same heading, and I edged gingerly to one side to fly exactly between two balloons ahead of us in that particular line. They were fairly wide apart and there was room enough but it felt rather a tight squeeze at the time.

Then, following the direction in which they were all

pointing, I eased between the next two, and then the next, with my eyes glued upwards and climbing as steeply as I dared to try and get above the brutes. I finally broke clear almost level with the last one, giving a cheerful and heartfelt 'All Clear' to the rest of my crew who had been suffering in silence while I had been juggling cautiously to get out of it. I realised that I was soaked with sweat as we settled down on course and began to relax, although there had been no physical exertion at all. Quite the opposite in fact as I felt almost as if I had been on tip-toe.

The rest of the trip was a piece of cake by comparison. A long stooge over the sea followed by a short run over enemy territory for a change. As the docks and whole target area were completely covered in fog on arrival there, we bombed through the usual barrage of flak on ETA and turned for another quiet run home. We landed at Driffield for some reason I cannot remember probably fog at Middleton – returning to our own base the next morning.

One good thing resulted from our experience though, in that we came to an arrangement with the balloon commander that the Middlesborough barrage would be hauled down to 500ft during our take-off and landing times in future. We had quite enough to worry about without having that hazard on our doorstep during those particular moments.

We were certainly back in the thick of things as a number of dicey incidents occurred at around this time, and always – it seemed – when it was my turn for OC night flying. The first was not too hair-raising, but it shows the sort of silly things which could occur. The sergeant pilot of a Halifax reported over R/T immediately after take-off that there was no airspeed showing on his ASI. The bomb aimer had then gone into the nose and seen that the pitot head cover had not been removed before taking off, so he must land again to take it off.

The pitot head was a small tube which protruded forward from the underside of the fuselage at the nose end. It had a small hole in the front, the wind pressure upon which then registered the air speed of the aeroplane on the indicator in the cockpit. A small electric element built into the tube ensured that this tiny passage was kept dry in the air and free from normal deposits of ice. It was not too easy to judge a landing of such a large aeroplane without the airspeed showing, even in daylight, but in the dark with a full bomb and petrol load it was that much more difficult, and consequently I had a harrowing few moments wondering if he could pull it off safely. He made a perfect landing however, had the offending cover whipped off, and took off again all in a few moments. These small covers were put on whenever an aircraft was on the ground to prevent grit or moisture from getting into the tube while the aircraft was grounded at dispersal.

The next incident occurred after the crew of a Whitley of 78 Squadron had radioed that they were returning to base early having received flak damage to their elevators while crossing the Dutch coast on the way out to a target in Germany. As their ETA approached, I ordered the crash tender and blood wagon to be standing by at the first flare, and waited in the control tower myself to speak to the pilot on their arrival. When they did come up on R/T, the pilot, Sergeant Woodhatch, repeated that they had been hit in the tail unit and that he had difficulty with the elevator controls. I told him to make a wide circuit and try to carry out a long, low approach to fly the aeroplane on to the ground if he could, and as slowly as possible with safety. A difficult manoeuvre under the best of circumstances. I then hurried out to the first flare myself.

The aircraft made a somewhat erratic approach but kept low as told. As it passed the first flare at only about 20ft up the pilot throttled back, but because he had insufficient control, the tail would not come down and the aircraft hit the runway in a nose-down attitude with an awful crunch. It did not bounce, but slithered forward only a few yards with a horrible rending noise and burst into flames as the ruptured petrol tanks spilled petrol on to the hot engines. I went out to it on the running board of the crash tender, fearing that the crew would be badly injured or worse and would have to be extricated, but moments later as we arrived at the burning wreck we soon saw that the crew were all out and safe, except the pilot who came staggering towards us injured, but very much alive, having been catapulted through the top hatch – naughty boy, he should have been strapped in.

I was astounded to see that he had a wide gash right across his forehead through which the bone of his forehead was showing, but amazingly no blood. The rest of the crew were quite unharmed because they had all been at their correct crash positions inside the Whitley, which proved the efficiency of sticking to the recommended procedures. The pilot too would have got out unscathed if he had been strapped in. Nevertheless he had done extremely well to fly an almost uncontrollable aircraft all the way back from the Dutch coast to make any sort of landing.

The crew were carted off to sick quarters where Woodhatch was stitched up and the others kept in overnight. The fire tender crew put the flames out, and the sad remains of the Whitley were dragged to one side of the runway so that our other aircraft could be landed when they returned.

Another incident also concerned 78 Squadron which seemed to be getting a run of bad luck at this time – more than its fair share in fact – which occurred at take-off on a really dark night. Several aircraft had got off quite happily, when a Whitley started its take-off run but suddenly throttled back when halfway down the runway, coming to a stop at what appeared to be right at the end on the perimeter track. From the balcony of flying control it looked as though the pilot was turning off the runway along the perimeter track to taxi round towards the starting point again, and keeping the flares on his left side. Meanwhile, before we could call him up on R/T to ask the score (RAF jargon for 'What the hell's happening?') the flare-path controller at the first flare had given the all clear for the next Whitley to trundle off.

Standing on the balcony watching events, it suddenly dawned on us there that the first Whitley was possibly still on the flare-path and had started to taxi back along the runway – a practice it was absolute RAF gospel to avoid at all costs. The Whitley taking off now had its tail well up with gathering speed halfway down the runway. It was too late to do anything, and we could only watch in horror as the inevitable collision occurred. The whole drama had taken only seconds to unfold from the moment when it became clear to the watchers as to what was taking place, far less time than the telling of it. There was an almighty crash and rending of metal, sparks flying, navigation lights dancing round in a ghastly waltz then suddenly separating and falling apart as two separate flickers of flame started and spread to create two separate bonfires as each aircraft caught fire. It was a terrible sight and quite obviously going to be even worse when we got out there.

I was on the way down the outside steps at the first impact, and chased after the crash tender and ambulance in the staff car. As we arrived at the wreckage and the rescue teams started, we found both crews already clear of their aeroplanes and miraculously without a scratch to any of them. Luckily the two aircraft had met port wing to port wing, and not head on as I had feared. They had then gyrated madly round in a half circle and been thrown apart by the speed of the impact, finishing up about 30 yards from each other on the runway.

By the time the crews were collected up it was obvious that the fires could not be got under control as at each fire there were about 700 gallons of petrol burning merrily away, so I ordered the crash tender crew to return to the transport section and refill the foam tanks. Moments later the petrol tanks exploded and both bomb loads blew up as well. So apart from the scattered and sad remains of two lovely Whitley aeroplanes, there were also two enormous craters in the middle of our main runway blasted out by the two bomb loads. We then had to signal our aircraft already in the air that they would have to land at other airfields after operations that night. The holes were filled in and re-surfaced within a day or two.

Towards the end of June, 76 Squadron was ordered to start practising formation flying by day which was not at all usual for heavy bombers and which had to be done of course between our normal operational requirements. It was something different to the daily run of our flying duties and much enjoyed by all the pilots, but which we had to take very seriously nevertheless, since it was clear that some special daylight operation must be in the offing which naturally gave rise to much speculation and not a little excitement.

On 3 July, however, I was promoted to Wing Commander and given command of 78 Squadron which was shortly to move from Middleton to Croft, a few miles away, where one of the new satellite aerodromes had been built and was nearly completed. Squadron Leader Walter Williams who had been my Deputy Flight Commander at Abingdon was posted in to take my place in 76 Squadron and continued with the formation flying practice already started. Although I was sorry in a way to miss the expected daylight operation as this would have been a new experience, I was more than compensated by getting a full command of my own, which I was naturally delighted to have since it meant promotion as well. No 78 Squadron was still equipped with Whitleys at that time.

The reason for the formation practice became clear very soon after when 76 Squadron joined all the other four-engined bomber squadrons then in existence in a daylight attack on La Pallice docks. A second German battle-cruiser had now arrived there, and both now required bomber attacks to try and keep them there. It was not a large force of Halifaxes, Stirlings, and Manchesters which attacked, since there were not many of these new heavy bombers in service yet, and in spite of having fighter cover, the casualties were fairly heavy, with Walter Williams among them. His aircraft had been attacked by fighters on the approach run which had upset their tracking over the target, so he very bravely turned to make a second run virtually on his own. They bombed successfully this time but were again attacked by fighters, and this forced him to put the aeroplane down in the drink. All the crew got safely into the dinghy and were picked up by a French fishing smack, but were transferred to a German navy patrol boat before they had time to try and get away, spending the rest of the war in POW camps.

Perhaps my personal gremlins were looking after me still, since I missed that operation by virtually a few days.

It was a week or two before Croft Spa was ready enough to take 78 Squadron and it was during this spell that one of the new young pilots had tried to carry out a forced landing one night due to engine failure while on local flying practice. He pranged into a field some miles away and the aeroplane caught fire in spite of his having made quite a reasonable wheels-up landing. All the crew got out unharmed except for the pilot who had been stunned during the actual landing. He was pulled out by some of his crew and a brave local helper but not before he had sustained burns about the face and hands (the pilot, that is; the rescuers were all unscathed). Luckily they were only first degree burns and he suffered no lasting damage although I was quite shocked to see him when I went to the hospital the following day. His face was badly swollen and looked rather like a football with its gauze dressing covered in acriflavine, and I was pleasantly surprised when the doctor told me that it was not all that serious.

His poor mother was there, too, and in a very emotional state. She was on the elderly side and a rather frail, nervous type at that. Naturally she was completely unnerved at the situation and I felt desperately sorry for her. I believe that it was of some comfort to her in her misery that she was able to talk with one of her son's brother officers and his Squadron Commander at that. This was not a very happy start to my new responsibilities, but we moved over to Croft Spa a few days later and for the next six months we had remarkably few – if any – fraught situations, dicey moments, unnecessary prangs or other momentous occasions normally associated with any operational station in those days.

Except, that is, for the sudden descent of the AOC No 4 Group Air Vice-Marshal Roddy Carr who decided on a snap inspection of his newest station and first 'satellite' airfield at very short notice. But there had been a number of snags attending our move. We had been required to operate in the normal way with no special relaxations or time to settle down. There were certain pieces of technical equipment missing from the servicing hangar and bomb dump, with acres of bare earth in untidy heaps everywhere, and builders' rubble and left-overs still cluttering up the landscape. It was therefore necessary for me to concentrate on the sheer necessities of getting the operational and technical requirements working smoothly first of all. I had paid no attention at all to the more domestic details for which there was a Senior Administrative Officer with a small staff for the day-to-day organisation. Nevertheless I was in overall command and should have checked with him that all was satisfactory on that side of things as well.

Thus all went well while we went round the technical site and buildings, the aircraft dispersal sites, and the various mess halls etc., in spite of the barren terrain which had at least been tidied up since our arrival. But it was when the AOC asked to be taken round the dispersed sleeping sites that things began to go wrong. The airmen's barrack huts were as clean and tidy as could be expected under the circumstances as the Warrant Officer in charge of discipline was responsible, but the sergeant aircrew quarters were an absolute disgrace. No beds were made up and obviously had not been for the three weeks we had been there. The dust was inches thick over the floors of their rooms, with great rolls of fluff in all corners and under the beds. The stoves had dead ash filling the concrete hearths and spilling over into the rooms. Everything was as slovenly as it could possibly be. One sergeant was having a wash in the ablution hut and on being asked by the AOC how things were, told him that he hadn't had a bath or shower for three weeks as the water was never hot. Mark you, no complaint had ever reached me on that score, but it did not go down well as you can imagine.

The Station Commander from Middleton was with us of course as he was in command of both stations in fact, and he very gamely tried to take the blame by saying that it was his responsibility and that he should have inspected Croft before this himself. He would, Group Captain Tommy Traill was not one to try and dodge responsibility, and was a humane and likeable commander in all respects. In a way he was quite right, but I was the local commander as it were, being on the spot, and could not escape my share of the wrath from on high. When the AOC came back for another look a few weeks later, there was quite a different story to tell.

These satellite airfields were being pushed up by the dozen all over the country to house the ever growing air forces in general, and bomber forces in particular. They all now had proper runways and hard standings for the aeroplanes with a continuous perimeter track connecting all so that aircraft need never run over grass at any time. But we still had our gooseneck flares and glim lamps for illumination. They all had a main site where the technical workshops, one hangar, squadron offices and crew rooms, and headquarters offices were grouped together. There was a separate site for the various messes, and at least three different sleeping sites, all widely dispersed for safety against air attack.

Many of these satellite stations were built with Nissen hut accommodation, which those who experienced them found to be very cold and unpleasant in winter, with rivers of condensation streaming down the metal walls. And there were always the irrepressible jokers who would come back from the local pubs late at night and relieve themselves of a skinful of beer by peeing great jets on to the sides of the huts before rolling in to their own cubicles. To those inside it sounded as if it was raining 4in nails, and would awaken the enraged inhabitants who had sensibly retired earlier than the revellers.

The brick huts which became more usual in time, were a little bit better and not quite so cold or damp. Although one brick thick with flimsy roofs did not exactly constitute luxury living, they were at least a slight improvement on corrugated iron. And we managed with whatever we were given.

About eighteen months or so after this, they became full RAF stations with a full time Station Commander, adjutant, administration, and engineer staffs with everything needed to look after their squadron. Thus the Squadron Commander only had the flying side to concentrate on without the worries of the domestic organisation or major servicing matters to sidetrack him.

With that major irritation out of the way and the station settled down to normal operational routine, I managed to get a few more trips behind me. Two of the targets had to be bombed through low cloud, and it is interesting to note that my log book states that on one of them – Frankfurt – my wireless operator got a W/T Fix from the Butser station behind Portsmouth, showing us to be bang over the town as we ran in to bomb the flak concentration.

On another night while on a return flight from Germany I had the unhappy experience of seeing no fewer than five aircraft shot down around us in the distance over a period of about an hour while we were running up to the Dutch coast on the way home. It was grimly fascinating to see in each case the short burst of twinkling horizontal tracer – without any answering fire unfortunately so each must have been taken completely by surprise – followed by a small red fire, growing steadily into a larger red ball as seen from a distance. Then a slow, curving fall to a final vertical plummet earthwards as the stricken bombers disappeared into the haze below, or crashed burning on to the ground. Each incident happened so quickly, and I wondered each time if the crew had managed to bale out safely, as we ourselves droned on homewards knowing full well that there were other night fighters most probably stalking us too.

In clear conditions like this I would change height or alter course continuously to try and confuse the radar-tracking equipment carried in the enemy fighters or used by their ground controllers, and make it more difficult for them to plot and follow us. The Germans had by now got their night fighters organised into a highly skilled and deadly force which had already begun to take a steady toll of our bombers. God knows, they got enough practice during the many hours we had to spend flying over their territory on the way to, or coming back from, our targets inside Germany. Only about six months before, I had joked with my rear gunner when he suddenly called out to me over Rotterdam where we were attacking oil storage tanks, that there were three fighters behind us on the port quarter, and turning steeply to port I had seen three black bursts of flak not very far away. I wouldn't be joking again about night fighter reports after this night.

As though to confirm what we all now knew was being achieved by the Luftwaffe night fighter force and its controllers, there was a night when all our crews reported a very unusual weather condition over the Continent which caused very heavy losses to the Command and to our Group in particular. It was a full moon night, and the weather predictions were good for the whole of Germany. However, over the other side, while the weather was good enough, great areas of the ground were covered in either very low cloud or thick fog. Probably it was cloud and in only a thin layer at that, but which shone a bright white in the moonlight. Also, way up above there was another thin layer of alto stratus cloud which was not thick enough to hide or obscure the moon, but simply spread its light to cover the heavens with a bright white ceding illuminated almost to daylight standards by the full moon above.

Between these two bright silver-white layers it was almost as clear as day, giving the enemy night fighters a field-day with big successes under those freak conditions. The top cloud was both too high and too thin for use as cover, and the cloud down below was too low, so our bombers were trapped in a clear white limbo and heavy casualties resulted.

It had one result in that it forced a change of policy as to the future tactics of the Command. Up to this moment Bomber Command had endeavoured to operate at full strength and intensity throughout the full moon period in order to take advantage of the better visibility for target finding whenever the weather permitted. After this, however, no more maximum efforts during full moons were called for, nor deep penetrations entailing long flights over the north-west of Europe.

We had a most unusual incident during this period with 78 Squadron when one of our pilots radioed not very long after take-off on his way down England. He said that his aircraft had been struck by lightning which had seriously injured his rear gunner who had also been blinded, and that he was landing at the first available flare-path to get aid for the gunner as quickly as possible. This he did, and returned to Croft the next morning without his poor gunner.

It seems that they were flying through a very minor storm when a flash of lightning struck the rear turret. The gunner had been handling the guns at that moment and had received quite nasty burns to both hands as well as being blinded by the flash. Happily he fully recovered in due course, but I never again heard of an aeroplane or gunner being struck like that. It was not supposed to happen at all since all metal parts in aeroplanes are bonded specifically to prevent this occurring.

One of the extraneous hazards we suffered from occasionally in Bomber Command, was from our own East Coast convoys along the shipping lanes. They had received so much attention from enemy bombers during the Battle of Britain with sporadic attacks ever since, that their protective gunners were extremely 'trigger happy', to say the least. Quite understandably, they would fire at anything and everything anywhere near them without bothering to challenge in the normal way. This again was quite understandable since the time wasted in making any challenge could well be used by an enemy bomber to line up for a bombing run or torpedo attack.

We were of course notified at all briefings if convoys were expected to be in our flight path, and of their expected positions when we were due to cross our coasts both on the way out and back, so that we would not fly over them at under 5,000ft. But there were times naturally, when the convoys were not in their anticipated positions, or our own aircraft were navigationally adrift after long hours in the air. Or perhaps bombers were returning lower than 5,000ft because of weather conditions or damage, and inadvertently passed too close to a convoy, which would then open fire regardless.

We knew the reasons and accepted them, but it was very galling to say the least when approaching our own coast after flying for several hours in hostile skies, to be greeted suddenly by a barrage of flak from itchy-fingered matelots when just beginning to relax and anticipate a return to home and breakfast. Pilots would dive away smartly, pooping off the required colour of Very cartridge to prove that they were a 'Friendly', and would generally get away with it. But there were a number of occasions when the navy gunners scored with their first bursts and one of our bomber crews would be shot down into the sea.

This very thing happened to one of my crews one night when their Whitley received a direct hit from a convoy gunner while approaching the Norfolk coastline after a bombing sortie. The pilot, a sergeant with only a few trips to his credit and so still fairly new to the squadron, was not able to control the aeroplane because of the damage sustained. He had to make a hurried ditching which to his great credit he carried out so well that the whole crew were able to scramble safely into their dinghy absolutely according to the text book. But they immediately discovered that the dinghy had been punctured by shrapnel and would not inflate properly, so they were in a parlous position. The pilot said that he would set off to try and make the shore as he was a very strong swimmer, and would then alert the air/sea rescue services. As it turned out, he had to swim about 8 miles, and luckily the tide was going in or he would not have made it. Of course it was broad daylight when he at last staggered ashore and found help, when he was told that he had just walked through a minefield. The pilot was the only survivor because the rescue boats and aircraft could find no traces of the rest of the crew. A sad ending to a very brave effort by the pilot.

Another very unlucky accident had recently occurred to one of the 76 Squadron Flight Commanders too. Returning damaged from a sortie, and flying up England in poor weather with a dwindling petrol supply, he decided to abandon the aircraft as there was no flare-path in sight. All the crew baled out safely, but as he himself got away part of his parachute got entangled with the tail unit of his aeroplane and he was dragged to the ground with the crashing aircraft. I had given him his dual instruction on the Halifax, and we had since become good friends. This sort of unfortunate end to any airman in an operational squadron always seemed much worse somehow than being lost in battle over enemy territory, and we all were that much more affected by it.

My last trip with 78 Squadron was a long flight to Nuremberg. On the way back we were flying above fairly thick cloud which reached up to about 14,000ft although the target had been clear. We must have strayed a bit off track to fly over one of the heavily defended areas because we were suddenly subjected to very accurate predicted flak coming up at us through the clouds. It was not in barrage form, but aimed individually at us and followed us relentlessly as we proceeded through the area for about thirty minutes. It was most uncanny, without any searchlights because of the thick cloud, but with continual bursts of heavy flak thumping around us rather too close for comfort.

However, frequent changes in height and small alterations

of course seemed to keep them guessing, and we flew on into a quiet area unscathed, if a little tired from the mental and physical concentration required for the previous half hour. We were quickly relieved by a few bawdy comments and some back-chat from a relaxing crew, who nevertheless had to be reminded by me that we were not clear of enemy territory yet and still had quite a way to go before we could safely relax with our coffee and sandwiches.

A few days later I received a signal from Group HQ 'screening' me from any further operations. This was the term used for taking aircrew off ops for a rest. I had to remain with the squadron for another two months, however, for a successor to be appointed. This was because one of my Flight Commanders who was to be promoted to take command of the squadron had unhappily gone missing a few days before this was effected, so I had to wait until another Wing Commander could be posted in to fill the vacancy. I eventually took up my next appointment as Wing Commander Operations in 4 Group HQ as from 1 January 1942.

CHAPTER FOUR

Resting

A T 4 Group I was in charge of the operations room which was concerned only with the arrangements for each operation as it was ordered from Command, and for collecting all information from the stations in the group relating to their operational capabilities each day. So each morning after the previous night's flying we would receive the expected serviceability of aircraft and the number of full crews available for the next operation the coming night. The Group total would then be passed to Bomber Command HQ so that the C-in-C would know first thing on arrival in his own operations room the exact numbers of aeroplanes and crews he would have available, and with each group doing the same he could then formulate his plans for the night.

The target orders would soon be sent from Command, and we would then have to get all the relevant information together for our AOC – numbers required, routes, timing, bomb loads, weather etc – for his operations conference with all the Station Commanders over the 'scrambler' telephone, after the stations and squadrons had themselves discussed the operation half an hour earlier. The rest of the morning would be taken up with passing information to the stations for the briefing of the crews, such as the signals instructions, convoy positions, intelligence information, details of any other operations being carried out or 'spoof' attacks, if any. The teleprinters would then bring in the crew lists for each squadron's battle order, and these would be chalked up by squadrons on a huge wall board ready for entering up the take-off times when they started off.

From the moment we received the target information from Command, when the routes and target were set out on our large wall-map, the operations room was strictly out of bounds to all group staff unless they were actually on the duty roster or involved technically in one way or another.

Once all details had been passed to stations there was a lull until take-off time, when we were kept busy filling in the exact time each aircraft was airborne as they were telephoned through from flying control at the stations. Another long pause then while we waited through the night for the return, dealing with signals from 'early returns' or aborted sorties for whatever reason. Or keeping an eye on the weather if dubious conditions threatened and consulting the Station Commanders concerned if diversions seemed inevitable.

Then there would be a rush of activity in the small hours while all our aircraft were landing back, logging each one down in turn on our blackboard as their landing times were telephoned in from the stations, and finally marking in the unhappy word 'missing' against those who did not arrive back at all. From then on we would be receiving the debriefing reports from the intelligence officers at the squadrons, to prepare a report on the night's operation for the AOC when he arrived at 08.30 next morning. Group Commanders could not possibly be in the operations room every night because of their daytime commitments, but Air Vice-Marshal Carr did come in sometimes at crucial periods for special operations, and he frequently visited individual stations to see the take-off or return landings and debriefing.

It was all quite interesting for a while, but it became rather boring and stereotyped after a few months. I eventually asked the AOC if he would find me something a bit more exciting and less routine, possibly with some flying attached, and suggested that it might be a good idea for the occasional bomber pilot to be posted on to night fighters to bring our experience of the other side of the coin to help improve, perhaps, our own night fighter and intruder operations against the enemy.

Three unusual and more interesting events did take place while I was there, however, which helped to liven things up and reduce the monotony a little, two of which involved us in some of the planning and organisation. The first was when our

Whitleys of No 51 Squadron, then stationed at Dishforth, were detailed to carry a small Commando force to Bruneval in the north coast corner of France, for an attack on a radar station which had been spotted there, and from which our back-room boffins wished to extract a special piece of apparatus for comparison with our own radar technology. Wing Commander Charles Pickard commanded the squadron, and Major Frost[3] the Commando unit, and they carried out combined training for a period before the attack was made. The drop was spot on when the time came, and the Commandos carried out a highly successful raid on the radar installation which achieved all the objectives set for it, at a low cost in casualties. After the attack was completed, the Commandos withdrew to a nearby beach where they were met by the Royal Navy to be taken home by boat. This was the first example of a fully combined operation by all three Services, and brilliantly executed by all three at each phase.

The 'Thousand Plan' bomber raid on Cologne was the next excitement, when a force of 1,045 aircraft was scraped up from all sources for a demonstration of what could be achieved if the Command was given the numbers and resources being asked for by our new chief, Air Marshal Sir Arthur Harris. At a time when our front-line strength was still only about 500 aircraft, there was a grave danger – as Harris saw it at this point in the war that our new four-engined heavy bombers would be dissipated throughout other commands and theatres of war. And the new C-in-C wanted to show the world just what could happen if a large number of bombers were concentrated into one force.

'Butch' – as he was affectionately to become known among his aircrew a little later on – had arrived to take over the Command at the beginning of 1942 and was a strong advocate of the need for all-out strategic bombing of enemy war resources. He immediately started fighting for an adequate bomber force to carry out his War Cabinet brief, as he saw it.

[3]Later Commanding General of the Parachute regiment.

IV

The details of the arguments and wrangle which went on over this have all been aired before, and it is not necessary for them to be repeated here. It is enough to record that the Thousand Bomber Raid was successful enough to make the C-in-C's point, and the Command was saved to become the great striking force which continually carried the war to the enemy heartland almost every single night of the war. It was the only arm of the Allied Forces with the ability to do this, until we were joined by our gallant American counterparts of the US Eighth Air Force to do the same thing by day.

We had been able to raise all these aeroplanes by exceptional effort on the part of the ground crews in all the bomber operational and training groups who prepared every single available aircraft including the reserves held, from the Heavy Conversion Units now in being, from the Beam Approach Training Flights, and from all the OTU's as well. Special mention must be made of these, because their aircraft had to be withdrawn from training to be fitted with heavy bomb racks and other equipment not normally carried in the training aircraft, with the consequent tremendous amount of extra work necessary to prepare for this operation. The Staff instructors on 'rest' from operations, and the senior pupils nearly ready for posting manned these OTU aircraft.

Göring's promise to the German people that no enemy bombers would ever penetrate over the Fatherland had already long ago been thrown back in his teeth, and this attack was not only a shattering blow to the morale of their citizens, but also a practical indication to the German High Command demonstrating in no uncertain manner what could well start to happen to other towns. Hitler was furious and ordered reprisals, which took the form of a series of attacks on our Cathedral Cities in what became known as the 'Baedeker' raids, referring to a German Tourist Guide which gave details of British architecturally historic buildings and places of similar interest.

So this was my third excitement because York was

naturally on their list, and one night received the obligatory visit from three or four Ju88's on a bright, moonlit night. Our HQ offices and ops room were situated just outside the city in a delightful old country house. These types of edifice were ideal for the purpose, and were being used all over the country by various and assorted Government departments, all of them having several large rooms and many smaller ones, readily convertible for quick occupation when the national emergency arose. The owners, I suspect, had been only too delighted to lease these white elephants to the Government for 'the duration'.

When the raid on York started I was in my digs near HQ, not being on duty that night, so I flung on some clothes and ran to the ops room to check up on what was happening. This was pretty obvious anyway, so we went outside to watch the fireworks from the garden. Did I say fireworks? We saw the occasional Ju88 fly over at about 1,000ft only, and heard a few smallish explosions from the direction of the centre of the city. But there was no return fire from the ground as York was completely undefended, as were the other cathedral cities such as Canterbury, also visited by the Luftwaffe. I think that one single Vickers gun was pooped off by some keen type from one of the several army units in and around the city, but since these were all non-combatant or initial training units, they, like us, had no anti-aircraft defences at all. There was no need, and our defences of major industrial areas and ports etc. were thin enough as it was, without being stretched to try and cover non-industrial areas as well.

So the Ju88's had it all their own way, and those of us who had recently come from squadrons could not help wishing that we had been given a few jammy trips like this to enjoy, when we remembered the amount of attention we normally received over almost every target. It reminded me of when I had been on leave some months previously not far from Southampton, and had witnessed from about 8 miles away the Luftwaffe attack on that great port. A strong force of He111's and Ju88's had bombed from high level doing great damage to the centre of the town – not the docks or factory areas – and I had been appalled at the lack of defences for a major port and industrial complex: half a dozen searchlights at most and as few guns. We used to get very much more than that when barge-bashing early in 1941 over Boulogne or Ostend.

We learned next day that York had not been very badly damaged as it turned out, which really was to be expected from such a small force using quite small bombs and incendiaries, and only a limited area round the railway station was affected.

By this time the AOC had fixed me up with a posting, and I left York a few days later to take over the Chief Instructor job at Abingdon once again. Not quite what I had hoped for really, but it seemed very difficult to get out of Bomber Command once in it – other than in the usual way on operations of course! Quite understandable really, since the Command was now always short of experienced Squadron and Station Commanders, and with the planned expansion already beginning it was essential to keep hold of all those who had completed a tour of operations. Of course eventually the age of all Squadron and Station Commanders in Bomber Command became much lower, and a considerable number of young chaps in their early twenties were promoted to Wing Commander to command operational squadrons because of their flying records and general abilities. I myself had a young Squadron Commander aged only twenty-one, with two tours of ops behind him already, when I was a Station Commander myself at Lissett later on. Jock Calder survived yet another tour with the famous 617 Squadron after this, and stayed on in the RAF when the war was over. A fine young officer and a superb bomber pilot.

The CI at an OTU did not do very much flying himself, but could at least keep his hand in whenever he felt inclined. He was responsible to the Station Commander for the complete training and organisation of the crews in the various aspects of the air and ground syllabus, as well as ensuring the supply of serviceable aeroplanes to the flights. A suitable staff of Flight Commanders and instructors for crew training, and senior engineer and technical staffs for the general maintenance problems, made quite a complex organisation which had to be co-ordinated through the CI's office.

This was where all the members of the bombers crews met up for the first time, having come in from the various specialist initial training schools, and where they now became 'crewed-up'. Instead of just detailing crews to fly together, we tried to give them the opportunity of sorting themselves out, and mutually choosing amongst themselves who they wanted to fly with. And it worked very well, for once they had made their choice it was only quite rare for changes to be made. So while the pilots were learning to fly the heavy twin-engined bombers used at OTUs, the navigators and wireless operators were in another flight doing cross country exercises day and night with staff pilots, until they all joined up together in a Whitley flight for the final phase of their training. A crew spirit was very quickly engendered, so by the time they were ready for posting to an operational group for final conversion and training on the four-engined bombers, they actively disliked flying with anyone else, firmly believing that their own pilot was the best ever and that they themselves were the best crew.

To digress a little in order to illustrate this, a small but typical incident occurred some time later when I commanded another squadron and a new crew was detailed to fly with a different pilot for an operational sortie one night. Their own pilot had gone down with 'flu, and they all objected strongly at having to fly with another particularly as they had done one operation together. I had to be quite firm with them, explaining that this had to happen sometimes, and that the pilot who would take them that night happened to be very experienced. They had to accept the situation of course, but they didn't like it very much. The amusing part of the whole business was that the Flight Commander concerned had told me that he wanted that crew to do further training between operations as he was not quite happy with their standard anyway.

The job was interesting and full, with heavy programmes to be achieved in all weathers with the absolute necessity of getting the crews through the 'sausage machine' as some wag once called it, in the allotted time and to the required standard. There were few failures, which spoke volumes for the methods of selection of aircrew and the initial training systems developed by the RAF.

There were few serious or fatal accidents, which was surprising considering the amount of flying carried out, the inexperience of the new crews, the difficulties of keeping heavily committed aircraft serviceable, and the general pressures created by working at top gear most of the time. Our Whitleys stood up to the demands made on them very well, for which much credit must be given to the maintenance staff and ground crews. Although the rate of accidents at OTUs seems to have been quite high generally if post war information is correct, I cannot remember it being so at Abingdon during either of the periods I was there in 1940 or 1942.

There were two more 'Thousand Plan' bomber raids in fairly quick succession while I was here, sending, some 900 aircraft each time to the Ruhr and Bremen, with the OTUs being called upon again. But they were not so successful as the original one, largely owing to the weather, and no further operations of this sort were organised again. The upset to the training programmes was too great, and the losses to the OTU component had been higher than to the operational groups in these last two raids. The crews had acquitted themselves well, but it was felt that our aeroplanes were now below the standards required for first line bombing operations.

On one of these raids we lost a staff instructor, Squadron Leader Tomlinson and crew. He had been with me as a Flight Lieutenant in 10 Squadron in 1940/41. Another loss was our Station Commander, Group Captain Herbert Massey, a World

War I pilot who had very gamely decided to go with a crew to see things for himself. Both baled out safely and were taken prisoner. Herbert Massey had lost half a leg during the first war, and became the Senior British Officer at Stalag Luft III of 'The Great Escape' fame, when seventy-odd aircrew tunnelled their way out, only to have fifty of them shot in cold blood by the Gestapo on Hitler's orders.

One useful thing which came out of these experiences, however, was that the new crews for their final exercise before posting, were to be allowed to fly over France on leaflet dropping sorties – 'Nickelling', as it was coded. This was a very useful exercise and experience for them, since the French night skies were a lot more friendly than those elsewhere. It kept the French populace informed and lifted their morale, while allowing the operational squadrons to concentrate on the more urgent matters requiring their attention.

The great bugbear at Abingdon was that Group HQ was also on the same station with us. Group Staff officers were almost as numerous as the OTU instructors, and were inevitably swarming round the place at all times. If there were any problems relating to the training syllabus they would inevitably come to my office or our flights for the answers, rather than go out to one of the other units, so they were always breathing down our necks which was a nuisance.

During 1940 this had not been a problem at all. Air Commodore McNeece Foster, the then Group Commander, was a most human and understanding person, and his staff all seemed to consider themselves as members of the station (which they were), although being on the Group strength. But now there seemed to be a divide somehow, which was all a bit unfortunate, and did not make for a congenial working atmosphere. They were also in the mess always, since many of them lived in anyway, and we could not work up a station spirit of our own with Group around like that. It was as if we were the lodger unit, rather than the reverse.

The first brush I had was with their Squadron Leader Ops

Training over a flying matter, very much concerned with training. One of my Flight Commanders had suggested that instead of doing four or five separate night flights on certain practice bombing and navigation exercises in the syllabus, we should try and combine all of them in one long exercise at 15,000ft, thus giving the crews the benefit of flying at least once at normal operational height before passing out. It would also have the great advantage of conserving the flying hours on our over-taxed aeroplanes, reducing maintenance problems and servicing times as well.

I thought it a really bright idea and worth a trial at least. But the Group staff refused even to consider it for a trial, and the Squadron Leader Ops went so far as to tell me that a Whitley could not get to 15,000ft anyway. (He had done a tour on Wellingtons.) It made no difference to him when I patiently explained that Whitleys had frequently flown over the Alps at 17,500ft on their way to Italian targets with full bomb loads. They would have none of it. But we did it anyway whenever possible, and saved quite a few aircraft hours to the great joy of our engineering officer. The other OTUs should also have been given the chance to try it.

Another niggle occurred after the AOC walked across the aerodrome to his office one fine summer morning, from his house on the other side. This took him past the firing butts where a course of new air gunners was receiving instruction in the handling of the power-operated gun turret which carried four Browning machine guns. Three turrets were set up on jigs in the open and connected up to an electric power supply so that the trainee gunners could get the feel of a turret and learn how to manipulate one under power. Only three could get instruction at any one time therefore, and the remainder would sit or stand around, watching and listening and having a quiet smoke while awaiting their turn or having finished. The AOC had noticed their smoking, and immediately gave orders to all stations under his command that no smoking was to be allowed in future at the butts during lectures or practical demonstrations. All rather petty and unnecessary, I thought.

The last straw for me however was over a much more serious matter affecting the whole method of organising the training syllabus which had evolved during the winter of 1939/40 when the OTUs were first formed. We had started off at that time when the syllabus was first issued by attempting to operate a system suggested by the Air Ministry. This was to do a certain ground lecture or practical exercise, and then repeat it in the air the following day. Then the next lecture on the syllabus would follow, with the next air equivalent afterwards once more, and so on. This was fine in theory, but we very soon found it impossible in practice.

The British weather would not co-operate even in summer, and we very soon got far behind with the flying programme, and too far advanced with the ground training, and the whole syllabus was cocked up almost from the word go. And with the very first intake we had to hurriedly think again. We held a conference on the station where it was unanimously agreed by the Station Commander, the Wing Commander and all the Flight Commanders that the only way to get through the syllabus cleanly, was to go through the ground training lectures and practices in one concentrated and uninterrupted period of two weeks, following on with the air exercises and all the necessary flying practices as weather permitted for the next two months or whatever time was expected of us. In impossible flying weather, crews standing by for their air exercises would be given extra ground instruction or revision under flexible arrangements through the Chief Ground Instructor who was in charge of all ground training.

So it was that I had been personally involved with the development of this system right at the beginning after the formation of the OTUs in 1939, a system forced on us by experience and practice. It was no theory, and was accepted in toto by all the other OTUs and by the new Group Commander, McNeece Foster, as all the other stations had simultaneously come to more or less the same conclusions as we had. Even in the very bad winter of 39/40 we had got through our flying commitments in the allotted time, and it was really because of that bad winter experience that we had been forced to seek a more practical system than the one advocated by the authors of the syllabus.

Now in September 1942, the Group Commander suddenly called a conference of all his Station Commanders to consider a wonderful new system of working the OTU syllabus which one of his Station Commanders had recently put forward. As CI, I would not normally have attended, but we had a very new 'Station Master' at Abingdon who had replaced dear old Herbert Massey who had so recently gone missing on one of the 'Thousand' raids. Group Captain Adams asked the AOC if I could go along too since he had only just arrived from commanding an operational bomber station and knew nothing of the workings of OTUs, and I was allowed to attend. So there I was, a lone Wing Commander among a gaggle of Group Captains, with the Air Commodore presiding.

The few general items on the agenda were quickly dealt with, and then the AOC called on the particular Group Captain to explain the bright new ideas in practice at his station. Readers will have guessed already that the brilliant fresh concept now being explained so carefully, was none other than exactly the one we had discarded so rapidly three years previously. I just couldn't believe my ears at what I was having to listen to, and sat back at the end of the talk waiting expectantly for one or more of the other Station Commanders to start tearing the idea to shreds. But apart from one or two enquiries on very minor points, not one of them appeared to understand any of the true implications. I was astounded, and knew that it would be up to me to make the necessary objections.

So I whispered to my CO asking if he minded my saying something, and he told me to go ahead. So I got to my feet to explain to the conference that all this had been tried out before on the formation of OTUs three years ago, and found to be impossible to carry out in practice; that it might be ideal in places with perfect weather conditions like South Africa or America; that it would be impossible to get through a day's lectures starting at 08.30 hours after crews had been flying the night before until 3 or 4am and then needed a lie-in next morning; that it had not worked before so why should it now, and so on. And, finally, that to change over to another system – so different would in itself create more problems, and result in a long delay in completing the training of at least two courses of the current intakes.

The only comment that the AOC had to make to my objections, was that the crews on night flying would just have to start earlier next morning! He would not budge from his decision to make the change, and there was no discussion on the points I had raised. He asked the others for comment, but no one else had anything further to add. He asked the Group Captain who had put the scheme forward whether he had come across any of the snags mentioned, during the time the scheme had been running at his station, and the latter completely denied that there had been any so far. Consequently we were all ordered to implement the scheme with the next intake of trainees to come in.

Back with my own CO in his office after the conference, I once again voiced my strong misgivings, and suggested that I should fly over to the station concerned, and take our CGI to see exactly how they were managing it. He readily agreed, and we flew over the very next morning, going straight to the CI there to tell him of the conference the previous day, and asking to see his progress charts and syllabus schedules, etc.

'We haven't got any yet, as we are not ready to start,' was his astonishing reply. I said in amazement, 'But your Station Master told us quite emphatically yesterday that the scheme was working satisfactorily.' The incredible answer came back: 'Oh no, he's got it all wrong. We haven't even started yet.' So I told him in no uncertain terms, what a bloody silly idea it was, how it had been tried out already three years previously, and why it was completely unsuccessful. Then I stormed out to return to my own station, leaving him more than bewildered, and myself very angry.

Reporting the visit to my CO an hour later, I told him that I simply refused to revert to a damn silly system which I knew from personal experience could not be made to work, and he could have me posted away if he wished. But if I remained I would continue with the well proved organisation of the syllabus as now practised. Rather surprisingly, he agreed entirely with my attitude as he had immediately grasped the implications when I had spelled them out at the conference, and 'told me to carry on as we were, adding cautiously however that he himself knew nothing about it officially.

'But what about our progress charts and syllabus programming details when Group staff come round to inspect?' he warned.

I had already thought about that one and replied that I would show the existing progress charts and graphs etc., which were fairly complicated to an outsider anyway – each station having evolved its own method of recording progress, so there was nothing standard about them. And we would post up some sets of training schedules to make it look as though we were operating the scheme, so that they would be 'blinded with science' and go away happy. I told him that I was willing to accept full responsibility if I did not get away with the camouflage, adding that I was sure that the old RAF adage that 'Bullshit Baffles Brains' would preserve me from discovery.

He laughed and agreed that it probably would. Thank God for a sensible CO, I thought as I walked back to my own office with the good news for my CGI, Squadron Leader Woodroffe, and senior navigation instructor, Squadron Leader Forrest. Both had known me before in 10 Squadron, and neither wanted to change to another system.

Two or three months later when I was elsewhere, I noticed

with some despondency in the newspaper that the Group Captain who had initiated this farce had been awarded the CBE. Oh well! And I never did hear what happened eventually, although I would bet my bottom dollar that all the OTU's reverted very smartly as soon as possible to the well-tried and tested method they had been forced to abandon. Thinking about it later, I suppose that I should have put in a report after visiting the other station's CI and really stirred things up. But I was so browned off with the whole thing that it just about finished me with OTU Group HQ, and I quietly telephoned the Wing Commander i/c Postings at Bomber Command, without telling my CO, and asked him to find me an operational squadron, and something really interesting if possible. My official 'rest' period was over, but my seniority was such that I could probably have soldiered on at OTU by making myself a yes-man to Group, but this was not my style. And anyway I was missing the tremendous spirit and atmosphere of an operational station, so very different to that at Abingdon, situated as we were on Group's doorstep where I could engender no atmosphere of my own making, with so many HQ staff officers cluttering up the landscape.

At the beginning of October a posting did come through for me. On the 3rd I flew down to Chivenor near Barnstable in Devon, to take over No 51 Squadron which had been on loan to Coastal Command and was still flying Whitleys on long range anti-submarine patrols into the Bay of Biscay. It was time for the squadron to be returned to 4 Group from where they had been detached about six months earlier, to re-join Bomber Command and be re-equipped with the Halifax II. I was told that the squadron was in a somewhat unhappy state with morale suffering for some reason, and that I would have to pull it back into shape. To help me in this I could ask for any particular officers I wanted as Flight Commanders or specialist leaders. So I asked Flight Lieutenant Dinty Moore, who was then an instructor at Abingdon, if he would come with me as he was due for a second tour, and telling him that he would get promotion to Squadron Leader as well. He jumped at the chance to command a flight. I had known him previously in 4 Group when he was a Flight Sergeant Pilot, and he was a most efficient officer and first class pilot, an ex-Halton 'Boy' entrant into the Service which was always a recommendation anyway.

My old wireless operator from 10 Squadron also came along with me. He was instructing at Abingdon too, and I had come to appreciate even more his sound qualities and expertise at his job. Butch Heaton was delighted to re-join me, and I managed to get him a commission too, which he well deserved. He eventually became the squadron signals leader and made the rank of Flight Lieutenant before his second tour ended. All well earned. Butch had been a bricklayer before the war, and was a quiet, modest, efficient, and likeable man whom I was glad to have on the squadron.

I also asked for Squadron Leader Douggy Foreman from an OTU at Chipping Warden, but although he was very keen to come with me, his posting was stopped by his Station Commander who did not want to lose a good Flight Commander. As it turned out he lost him anyway, because, sad to say, he was killed soon afterwards while flying on a training flight with a pupil crew. It was a most unhappy circumstance because he might well be alive today if he had been allowed to join me, since all my three original Flight Commanders who came with me to 51 Squadron, survived their second tours safely. Such are the vagaries of fate. Douggy was a most cheerful and carefree type and I would have liked to have had him with me as my second Flight Commander. However, I was given instead a Squadron Leader John Russell whom I had not known before, and who had been instructing at one of the Whitley OTUs at Kinloss or Lossiemouth. He turned out to be a quiet efficient Flight Commander who did an excellent job in the squadron.

Arriving down at Chivenor with Dinty Moore and Butch Heaton, and after taking over from the outgoing Wing Commander whom I knew well, I soon found that any trouble there seemed to have resulted from the offhand treatment which everyone in the squadron felt they had received from the station personnel and Coastal Command in general, as the Coastal bods had apparently looked upon 51 Squadron as rather unnecessary interlopers, and they never seemed to have integrated properly. A pity, because they were all doing the same job, Coastal Command themselves having Whitleys at Chivenor.

How much, if any, of the blame could be placed on the squadron, I could not tell; nevertheless there was a bad atmosphere all round right through the aircrew to the humblest erk, which was unfortunate to say the least. Coastal Command had full operational and technical control of the squadron of course, and all their personnel, particularly on the station, should have done everything in their power to make a guest unit feel at home.

Matters were made worse when one of the 51 Squadron crews reported having had a running battle in the middle of the bay, when they were attacked by three Arado floatplanes, much used by the Germans for coastal defence against low-flying reconnaissance aircraft.

The rear gunner, who was also the gunnery leader, Flight Lieutenant Buster Storry, so conducted the ensuing dog-fight together with his pilot that they not only avoided being shot down into the drink, but claimed that they had destroyed two of the attackers and driven off the third which was damaged and forced to retire. No one was put up for an award which was richly deserved by two of the crew at least if their story was true, and which the whole squadron firmly believed even though Coastal Command did not, apparently.

However, most of the squadron had brightened up when they knew they were returning to their old group, and after sorting out who was to go for the Heavy Conversion Course, and who for rest, everyone had some leave, and reported afterwards to the HCU at Pocklington, or direct to Snaith in Yorkshire which was to be the squadron base from then on.

All the maintenance crews went to Pocklington as well to familiarise themselves with the layout and installation differences of the engines and airframes. I was at Snaith with the adjutant and office staff to prepare the paperwork, and for the descent of the rest of the personnel when the conversions were finished. The old Whitleys were flown away to OTU's or storage depots, and our new Halifaxes started to arrive plus some of the ground crews to look after them. An instructor from Pocklington flew to Snaith one morning to give me a refresher flip of some circuits and bumps, and the whole squadron was assembled at Snaith and ready to operate by 1 January 1943.

CHAPTER FIVE

Bomber Ops Later Style

IT was just a year since I had left 78 Squadron and although some operational procedures and practices had begun to change from the middle of 1941 on, that was nothing compared to the much more professional approach now evident. The rather haphazard and individualistic attitudes had disappeared entirely, which was absolutely necessary having regard to the tempo and numbers which had increased quite considerably during that one year.

Up to mid-1941, for example, a Station Commander could telephone the AOC at Group and ask if he could have his stand-down night arranged for a certain date as there was to be a mess party on that night, and it would be granted. Mark you, it could only be done perhaps twice in a year, but still it occurred throughout the whole group. I can remember one night at Leeming early in 1941, coming back from a bombing sortie and going straight into a sergeants' mess dance after debriefing. The dance had not been cancelled in spite of our flying requirement that night. Ah, slap-happy days. But no longer, thank God.

Now, twelve to sixteen aircraft would take off at one minute intervals for a mission, and this soon became eighteen to twenty-four when we got our third going a few weeks later. This was unheard of eighteen months before when six to ten aeroplanes might take up to forty minutes to get airborne, as a speedy take-off was not necessary in those days.

Now, taking off to set course as quickly as possible was absolutely obligatory in order to achieve the necessary bomber stream concentration which was a vital tactical necessity for our aircraft over enemy territory in order to try and swamp the enemy defences, making it more difficult for flak and night fighters to be directed individually on to our bombers.

Landing back at base was also much faster. We could now get twelve aeroplanes landed safely in perhaps twenty

Group Captain A.V. 'Tom' Sawyer
DFC

A crew of 76 Squadron leaving their Halifax

Two Whitley bombers of 10 Squadron making for enemy territory

76 Squadron Halifax

A Halifax of 51 Squadron shown during an attack on an oil plant
Wanne-Eickel in the Ruhr

minutes or so, at about two minute intervals by night, whereas previously half a dozen aircraft might well have arrived home over a spread of two hours or more, if the target had been at any distance or the forecast winds badly out. All of this had been made possible by the advent of the 'GEE Chain', which made such a vast improvement to our navigation. I would go so far as to say that this was the greatest single improvement to our navigational aids during the war, and which lasted until the automatic systems were introduced well after hostilities ceased.

It was a tremendous asset, and very reliable, with minimum failures, seldom letting us down. It was accurate to about 250 miles, so at last our navigators could get continual and accurate position checks well on the way to the targets, and just as important, also find accurate positions when on the way home, even above cloud. Of course, the enemy soon found ways of jamming the system, so that it became less useful when actually over enemy territory, but a good start could be made on the way out, and a safe landfall coming home. The result was that nearly all aircraft now reached the correct target, and there were many fewer losses from tired aircrew not being able to find their way home. An end to the dreaded 'dead reckoning' hit or miss method meant no more swanning out over the Irish Sea over cloud with a duff wireless set and lousy wind forecasts.

Without getting technical – which I couldn't anyway because it was as much a Black Magic system to me as any other highly technical gadgetry – it enabled the navigator to obtain very accurate position 'fixes' through special radar equipment which gave him a much more precise pinpoint of his air position at any required moment.

Taking several of these at regular short intervals, the navigator could then work out a wind for himself from his true course, track and airspeed, and thus check if the forecast winds were correct or not.

Several other things had changed as well by now. With the

Americans over here in large numbers their influence was being felt. Wireless sets had mysteriously been turned into 'radios' (and were much more reliable by now too). The word aerodrome was old hat, the complex now termed a 'base' and the landing area being an 'airstrip' or 'airfield'. The watch tower or control tower had now become 'flying control tower' or simply 'flying control', and instead of asking for permission to land, you merely said, 'May I pancake' (for some completely inexplicable reason). We also had to change to the USAAF style of alphabet for R/T chat which took a little getting used to, for instead of A – Apple, B – Beer etc. it became A – Able, B – Baker, to name but two, and although there were a few of the old words still left in, several more most unlikely words appeared at intervals throughout the alphabet. R/T drill was much shorter too, messages no longer being repeated unless asked, and 'Over to you – Over' now condensed to simply – 'Over'. 'Message received and understood' became just 'Roger' – (for 'R' – received).

All this was very necessary when there were anything from twelve to twenty-four aeroplanes all arriving 'upstairs' over the airfield within moments of each other, and being stacked at 250ft height bands as they called up in turn, until brought down tidily and carefully to land at two minute intervals. So R/T discipline and circuit regulations had to be tightened up considerably. No longer would the comedian of the squadron be allowed to get away with curious or deviational chat over the R/T on arrival, such as the comic in 10 Squadron very early on who called up from his Whitley – 'Hullo Control – this is Rabbit P for comfort here. May I have permission to land please?' We had to be as brief and orderly as possible to keep the air clear for the next chap, and more importantly for anyone in real trouble. Now it would have to be just – 'Rabbit P Peter calling control. May I pancake?'

The airfield lighting arrangements had undergone a big change as well. Gone were the glim lamps and gooseneck paraffin flares (although the latter were kept as a stand-by for failure of the power supply, or for additional lighting in misty conditions). There was now a permanent installation of electric lighting which had become standard for the whole RAF, and from which was developed the airfield lighting system for all present day service and civil airports. It was known as the 'Drem System', because it had been invented and first tried out at Drem in Scotland where another bomber OTU was situated.

Each of the three runways was lit along the whole length and on both edges with electric lights set flush with the ground. A funnel of lights at the ends of all runways could be switched on individually to denote the down-wind end of the runway in use, and known as the 'lead-in funnel'. At the ends of each runway, and sited on the left side only – as approached from the air – was an instrument 'borrowed' from the Royal Navy who had used it for some years already as a most useful visual aid to pilots making landings on aircraft carriers.

This 'Angle of Glide Indicator' was a beam of three lights projected towards landing aircraft: yellow on top, green, red. If a pilot saw the yellow he was too high, green showed that he was safe, red that he was too low, and had to gain height.

Add to this the blue lights which edged the perimeter track all the way round on both sides for aircraft taxiing to or from dispersal points, and finally the whole area surrounded by a vast circle of white electric lights set on posts in the fields around the runways, then it can be seen that this was indeed a great step forward. The whole system was controlled from the flying control tower, where an illuminated repeater map showed the complete lay-out in a miniature plan. All duty personnel there could thus see at a glance which lights were on, which runway was in use etc. and the controller could make any alteration at the flick of a switch, have reduced lighting if wanted, or turn the whole lot on or off at once if necessary.

On clear nights, these great circles of light could be seen all the way up England from the coast, although in murky weather if one was lost or otherwise in trouble, and looking for a quick landing, it was amazing how they mysteriously disappeared.

There were two small but important items among all the changes. First the escape kits issued before every operation were all neatly packed into a flat perspex box about 6in x 4in x ¾in which held the silk maps, money, benzedrine tablets, malted milk concentrate in tablet form, and a sort of miniature hot water bottle for drinking water, with a supply of purifying tablets if the only water supply available to someone on the run was river or ditch water. All sealed up with sellotape or its equivalent, this had to be handed back intact at debriefing of course. The other change was that aircrew were now issued with sets of combination underwear for flying. Made of fine wool, these Long Johns were extremely warm and comfortable, and except for the rear gunner, meant that the cumbersome Sidcot suits or the newer Irvine jackets need no longer be worn. Our aircraft were better heated than before too, all of which made the crews that much more comfortable and uncluttered.

Finally, the aircrew buses needed for taking the crews to and from their aeroplanes at dispersal, were now especially designed for the job, no longer requiring the undignified scramble to get into the back of an open lorry. And of course all the transport required for servicing and maintenance was now standardised and of official types, as opposed to the motley collection of assorted requisitioned vehicles we had worked with at Leeming in '40/41.

Thus, with the equipment and organisation so much improved, the Command build-up, which had started in earnest during 1941, was by now gathering pace with the numbers of front line aircraft and crews increasing almost weekly. But the enemy were not going to be left behind. Their night fighter organisation had been enormously improved with all the practice they were given by us, and they had to divert a very high proportion of their war effort to the production of fighter aircraft, as well as huge numbers of men and women for air raid precautions, fire fighting services, street clearance, and repairs to public utilities after air raid damage.

So the night skies above Germany had become extremely unhealthy and much busier, and it was from the middle of 1942 onwards therefore that most of the outstanding feats of endurance and bravery took place, and not a few examples of fantastic luck as well. Much has already been written about the hairy exploits which took place in those unfriendly skies, and it would take volumes to collect and relate every one. It is not the purpose of this book to do this, and only a few will be mentioned to illustrate the sort of atmosphere in which bomber aircrew lived and worked. There are other stories too, of some of the luckier ones who managed to survive crazy and impossible situations. But to put the record straight, there were also a few incredibly lucky crews who somehow managed to sail through a whole tour of operations without a single dicey moment and never receiving any damage at all even through the toughest times from the autumn of 1942 to the autumn of 1944, while others were coming back several times with heavy damage after dreadful experiences or not coming back at all of course.

I myself was never attacked by a night fighter, although I did once see a Focke Wulf 190 fly right across our path about 70 yards ahead on a bright moonlit night, and had to dive away smartly down moon to give him the slip. And although there were three or four occasions when I thought we might be for the 'chop' and others when we received some slight flak damage, I never received really severe damage or engine failure entailing a dodgy homeward journey to 'come in on a wing and a prayer' as the war-time song so dramatically put it, and so I was among the luckier ones too.

There were two examples of the most amazing good luck: the first when a sergeant rear gunner abandoned the rear turret of a Lancaster without his parachute. The aircraft was a blazing inferno and the gunner's 'chute was held in a special container just inside the fuselage behind the turret. When he tried to reach for it, he found that it was burning merrily away too, and quite useless. So he decided that he would rather die suddenly by hitting the ground than by being cooked alive in a burning, crashing bomber, and calmly turned his turret round pushing himself out backwards in the approved fashion. However, it was winter, and although the height from which he started his fall was 18,000ft, and the terminal velocity of a human body draped in flying kit is roughly 120mph, he had the astounding good fortune to crash through the tops of some fir trees which slowed his rate of fall, and thence into a very deep snow drift. Although temporarily unconscious he was only comparatively lightly hurt. The Germans who captured him would not believe his story at first, and made a thorough search for his 'chute thinking he had buried it. Only when they found his burned parachute where he said it would be in the burnt-out aircraft, did they then corroborate his story and believe him.

The other luckiest ever escape happened to an Australian Flight Lieutenant who was captain of a Halifax. The aircraft had been attacked by a night fighter and the petrol tanks were on fire. He ordered the crew to bale out, but before he had time to clip his own 'chute on, the aircraft exploded and he was blasted out into the open at a height of 17,000ft. But he had not fallen far before he landed plumb in the middle on the top of the fully opened parachute of a member of his crew, descending together precariously like this until both landed quite safely. An incredibly lucky fluke for the pilot.

At least once it had been reported that two members of a crew had jumped out of a crashing bomber clinging together under one 'brolly' because the other's had been destroyed, and had landed successfully. It is also known that two men tried this on another occasion, but the jerk and sudden deceleration created by the opening parachute had caused the one who was desperately hanging on to lose his grip and fall to earth.

Among the more interesting jobs falling to Bomber

Command, was the control and operation of what we used to call the 'Cloak and Dagger' squadrons. From an aerodrome at Tempsford in Bedfordshire, they used a variety of aircraft such as the three-seater Lysander which could land on a pocket handkerchief – Hudsons, Whitleys, Halifaxes, Stirlings, and Warwicks. They did most interesting work flying secret agents to the various underground movements on the Continent; dropping arms, ammunition, supplies, radios etc; picking up and changing agents in lonely fields dimly lit by torches held by members of the local Maquis, and so on. It was not all that dicey by normal bomber standards, as they usually flew low to undefended areas, picking their routes carefully to avoid detection both for themselves and for the brave people they were 'visiting'. But there were of course some hairy moments when caught by sudden bursts of light flak if straying over alert gun emplacements, when they were extra vulnerable for short, sharp spells, owing to being so low. The greater danger was to those heroic agents and wireless operators – men and women – who risked torture and violent death if they were caught. And many were, although there were always more to take their places when this happened.

One of the most outstanding stories of the many that occurred during these operations concerned a Norwegian agent who was parachuted into his own country one night, but made an awkward landing and put a knee out of joint as a result. He passed out and lay unconscious in the snow for a while, and when he came to and realised what had happened, he dragged himself to some trees and searched for a strong double sapling forming a close 'V' shape. He then jammed the heel of the injured leg into the fork, and thrusting away from the tree with his good leg, threw his whole weight backwards with as much force as possible, to try and re-set the dislocation. He actually succeeded in this, but passed out again with the pain. When he recovered once more, he made a rough splint with two stout sticks bandaged round with the silk cords cut from his parachute canopy, and then with the aid of a simple home-made crutch, he finally hobbled off to find his friends. Such was the stuff of those gallant agents.

A much more light-hearted episode with a happy ending – but nevertheless a bit fraught while it was happening – occurred one night while I happened to be visiting Tempsford on my way south on leave, to see my old friend Charles Pickard. He commanded one of the squadrons there at the time, and was flying that very night, taking a Hudson to some out of the way field deep in the middle of France to put down two or three agents with some supplies, and to pick up another three who were due to return home. He took me to the dressing hut where the agents were preparing, and then to flying control where I watched a couple of Halifaxes go off on their nefarious duties of arms dropping, followed by Charles in his Hudson.

After a meal in the mess, I went into the operations room to await events but at the appointed hour when we should have received the radio code-word for 'operation completed' to show that he was on his way home, nothing was heard. Dead silence from the signals section. We kept on waiting amid deepening gloom, and everyone imagining that the worst had happened, when suddenly, and hours late, the code signal was received and our spirits lifted again. But it was getting on for daylight and he was still well inside France. Another signal soon after asked for fighter cover to be laid on for when he reached the French coast in full daylight. This was arranged with Fighter Command, and he eventually arrived safely at Tempsford.

Until his signal had been received, we had all feared that he and the agents had flown in to a reception committee of the Wehrmacht instead of the Maquis. But it transpired that they had arrived at their field and landed safely enough, deposited their cargo of agents and supplies and taken on the return party all in record time, only to find that while all this had been going on the aircraft had become bogged down to the axles in soft ground, and they could not get out.

They tried to dig channels in front of the wheels, having had to scrounge round the area for spades of course, then revving up the engines to full power to try and drag themselves out by brute force. That did not work, and what with the noise they had been making and the interest being taken by the local population, the situation was becoming somewhat dodgy. Then a local farmer volunteered to go and fetch some cart horses, when with the aid of some stout rope and much heaving and shoving, the reluctant Hudson eventually came unstuck and they were able at last to take off without further ado.

But to return to Snaith where 51 Squadron was all set and raring to go, it was not until 3rd or 4th of January that we were called for the first time, as a spell of really bad weather had set in. So after an early stand-down one morning, I laid on a squadron party for that night in the camp gymnasium, at which the aircrew would entertain the ground crews, which I thought might be quite a useful morale booster. The aircrew all thought it would be a marvellous idea, so at about 20.00 hours, we all gathered at the gym as per arrangements, where the Naafi manager had installed several barrels of beer and provided some sandwiches. It was a freezing cold night, and the iron stove at the end of the gym was roaring away, but only warming those who were lucky enough to get within a few feet of it. So after a time, our tankard-clutching hand became almost frozen in a claw-like position, and we had to prize the mug away for a refill and use the other hand in turn, which we kept suitably thawed for the purpose in a trouser pocket.

Nevertheless the whole evening was a great success. The senior NCO's of the technical branches – and of course the troops – being highly pleased at the compliment, and it really did start a squadron spirit going. Because all the aircrew and ground staff had recently been away training for about six weeks, this was a good method of getting them together. All the beer was finished to the last thick dregs without any blacks being put up by anyone, and of course the sandwiches were scoffed in the first few minutes as if a plague of locusts had settled.

I was much amused when in the general mêlée at the height of the celebrations, a Waaf sidled up to me and explained without any preamble at all that she had been the girlfriend of a previous Wing Commander at the station and would it be a good idea if I took her over too, as it were? If I hadn't had a few beers by then I would probably have been completely stymied, but as it was I didn't bat an eyelid, acting as though this was quite a normal sort of conversation. I explained gently and firmly that even if I were to consider any liaison of this nature, I would prefer to be away from my own doorstep so to speak, but thanks for the kind offer anyway. Face was thus saved all round.

When I presented the bill next day to the assembled aircrew in the crew room for a collection to be made, it was greeted with shouts of laughter, and no small wonder. The Naafi bill stated quite simply: 'To Beer supplied, £46.18s 9d. To Food supplied 16s/4d.' (At the present day equivalent of about 4p per pint, this was a fair amount of beer!)

The weather cleared the next night and we were off, putting up about eight crews on 'Gardening' sorties along the Danish and NW German coasts. This was the code-name for the sea mining operations as previously mentioned, and which Bomber Command had to carry out from time to time. They were considered by the authorities to be a reasonable sort of target for new crews to cut their teeth on, and were generally favoured by the crews who looked on them as being fairly easy. But they were not quite as healthy as all that, and a number of losses occurred on those operations.

Since it was our 'Opening Night' as it were, the AOC came over to see us off and have a look at his new station which had recently been taken over from 1 Group in the general re-hash when the Canadian No 6 Group was formed at this time, using the northern stations of 4 Group. There was a pre-dusk take-off which was fairly leisurely since all aircraft were going to different places, and while this was going on we were all standing in the control tower looking out across the runways taking in the general activity.

One aircraft had just taken off in its turn, with another taxiing round the perimeter track towards the take-off point and about to swing round on to the runway, when at almost the same moment we all saw a Halifax at nought feet over the far boundary hedge and approaching straight at us across the runway in use. Two engines on the same side were stopped, and its wheels were up, the two good engines screaming in maximum boost with the throttles obviously 'through the gate' as it was called when full emergency power was applied.

It was of course one of our own coming in to land in a hurry, but the poor pilot had been too busy fighting with the controls to call us up on R/T so this was the first we knew of anything untoward having happened. And it was aiming straight for the control tower with a mine still aboard and a full load of petrol. We all watched mesmerised as it made a wheels-up belly landing, tearing straight across the runway where another Halifax was just about to take off. With a rending of metal, and the sandy soil being sprayed up each side, it finished up a few yards away from a maintenance building, and only 30 yards to one side of the control tower.

Of course we all feared that the petrol would catch fire and explode the mine, and before it had stopped moving even I was down the outside stairs and up to the aircraft with the Station Commander and the AOC close behind. The crash tender crew were already there playing the chemical hoses on to the hissing and steaming engines, with the ambulance standing by. Luckily the fuel tanks were not ruptured and no fire resulted, and as I arrived the crew were already scrambling hurriedly out of the hatches. The mine had been wrenched off the bomb rack and was protruding half out from under the fuselage, and looking for all the world like a pregnant whale having a miscarriage. The mine had not been detonated by the impact and so had not exploded, but the whole event was somewhat exciting, and a hell of an exhibition to put on for the AOC's visit.

When we had learned from the pilot – a sergeant, and quite new, on his first sortie – that two engines had cut dead very shortly after he had taken off, the AOC gave him a personal pat on the back for excellent airmanship in getting the aeroplane down safely if somewhat dramatically in a very difficult situation. Definitely a good show on the part of the pilot.

A few days later, following more operations, we were sent details of a very special target for attack the next day involving a dawn take-off. Set for 12 January we were briefed in the late evening of the 11th for a daylight attack on the *Tirpitz* which had been discovered lurking in a Norwegian fjord, and which therefore posed a serious threat to our Russian convoys. The whole of Bomber Command was detailed to take part in this operation, and the flight plan was for 4 and 6 Groups to rendezvous over Flamborough at a set time and height band, then set course across the North Sea in a close gaggle for mutual protection at the other end when fighter attacks could be expected.

This was fine in theory and would have been equally good in practice, except for the weather – as usual. We were in the throes of a depression which apparently was going to last for at least another twenty-four hours and which was giving conditions of solid cloud from 1,000ft to 20,000ft and running miles out into the North Sea. Severe icing was also expected from 3,000ft upwards. Hardly the sort of weather to enable some 250 aeroplanes to go milling around in such a limited area. Why the operation was laid on at all under those weather conditions and forecast it is hard to imagine, because it looked so hopeless from the start. I suppose the *Tirpitz* had just arrived there and we needed to catch it quickly if possible. But we were committed to an 08.30 hours take-off next morning when it would still be quite dark owing to the fact that single summer time was in operation all through the winter during the war years.

We all went to bed after briefing, and the station was sealed off from the outside world for security reasons. No private telephone calls – in or out – no one allowed off the station etc. I could not sleep properly because of my misgivings. Although I was really looking forward to the operation itself, the thought of all those aeroplanes concentrating in a small part of East Yorkshire and all trying to reach Flamborough Head at the same moment in such weather, absolutely appalled me. I was filled me with dread because of the great risk of many mid-air collisions, which to my mind was an unacceptable hazard to ask of our crews.

My batman roused me from an uneasy half-sleep at 06.00 hours and I went straight to flying control with the Group Captain to get the latest information from the Met officer. A miserable cold drizzle was falling, and the weather situation was exactly the same, yet the operation had still not been cancelled. We all breakfasted rather quietly for once, went down to the flights, and on out to our aircraft at dispersals. Engines were started up all round the airfield, and still no word, everyone expecting the 'ops scrubbed' call every second.

I taxied out to the runway, turned into the wind, trod hard on the brakes and ran each engine up in turn testing the magnetos, and with my head down in the 'office' carefully checked the dials and carried out the last minute cockpit drills. The flight engineer was doing the same, and the bomb aimer was with me doing his part of the cockpit checks. So none of us noticed the red Very cartridge fired from the control tower which was the recall signal for Ops cancelled. I imagined that I had caught a glimpse of something for a split second, and paused for a moment expecting another to be fired off. Nothing further happened, and since R/T and wireless silence had been ordered I could not call flying control to ask for news. So with great foreboding for all my crews, and utter incredulity, I opened the throttles and took off, meeting the cloud base at only 300ft. Setting course for Flamborough I was determined to keep as free as possible from other aeroplanes, and stayed at 1,300ft which would keep us just clear of the Yorkshire moors *en-route*, and hopefully below other aircraft.

Of course the W/T coded signal for the cancellation came through within minutes, and we turned gingerly for base still believing that there would be a number of other aircraft all milling about in the 'clag' in the same predicament as ourselves. The whole crew was as tense as I was, and half expecting a rending crash at any moment in the now greying cloud. Down to 300ft again circling the airfield just below cloud, I was relieved to be told in answer to my query, that no other aircraft had taken off.

Because of the low cloud and poor visibility which still prevailed, I decided to dump my bombs in the sea off the Lincolnshire coast and not risk a landing in those conditions with a full bomb and petrol load. At the coast the weather was a little brighter and the cloud base slightly higher, but we still had to return at low level, just skimming over the Lincolnshire wolds on the way back to keep below the cloud, and landing back at Snaith quite safely after two hours and forty-five minutes of sheer messing about.

The Station Commander greeted me by saying that he was surprised at my mild demeanour, as he had expected me to tear off my helmet and stamp it into the ground with rage as I climbed out of my Halifax and into his car. He told us that the 'Scrub' had been ordered at the last possible moment, and they had only been able to get off one Very cartridge before I had taken off. After this we agreed that two cartridges should be fired off in quick succession under similar circumstances in future, and that R/T silence would be broken with an innocuous broadcast such as 'All training aircraft stand by' or something similar.

It had been an infuriating episode for me. It wasn't the two hours or so of flying in ropey conditions that mattered, but the anticipation of multiple collisions in cloud if all those aircraft had taken off which affected me most of all, plus the hours of anxiety we had all been subjected to so unnecessarily. Bomber crews had quite enough mental pressures to contend with in the normal course of our duties, which we were all prepared for and accepted, but to impose twelve hours of extra stress because of a weather hazard – which in this case was much worse than the expected normal bombing hazards of the operation itself – was really inexcusable.

The operation having been cancelled, it was not ordered again since security had been prejudiced and secrecy lost. As I have just mentioned, after all briefings now, each station was virtually sealed off from the outside world until the time of the attack for that night. Not like the old days when it was said that on any night when there were operations a full briefing could be got in the Half Moon, The Castle, or Betty's Bar in York from about 7pm onwards!

At about this time, the Halifax II had become somewhat unsatisfactory as far as those who had to fly them were concerned. The extra equipment we had to carry – Gee – H2S – radar jamming device against enemy fighters – greater petrol and bomb loads etc. were all adding extra weight to our aeroplanes which the original Merlin engines were now too underpowered to cope with. The final straw was the exhaust shrouds which had been fixed over the stub exhausts on each side of the four engines to shield the red hot glare from the enemy night fighters who could see them from quite a distance once their radar brought them fairly close.

All these things combined to reduce our operational height, and consequently we were always flying well below the Lancasters and receiving more than our fair share of attention from enemy flak and fighters. This was showing up in that the loss rate of Halifaxes ran at a higher percentage than the Lancs at that time. Our Halibags were also being showered with incendiaries from the Lancasters on occasions, pattering heavily all over our aeroplanes in a most unwelcome manner. Add to this the occasional bomb suddenly arriving inside the fuselage from above, and the resultant alarm and despondency caused to the crews on the receiving end can readily be understood.

One Halifax crew came back one night having received a heavy calibre bomb which entered the top of the fuselage just aft of the mid-upper turret, much to the indignation of the gunner ensconced therein, and which carried on straight through the aeroplane leaving a gaping hole at the port wing root. The pilot, Flight Sergeant Cameron, flew his crippled bomber back to base and made a safe landing after a somewhat draughty and uncomfortable return flight. Surprisingly no one was hurt. Another Halifax reported having a 500lb bomb suddenly appearing through the roof and remain lying about inside the fuselage. Two of the crew had to open the side hatch and roll the damn thing out.

So something had to be done to improve the Halifax, and the Mark II-Z appeared. This had the small front turret above the bomb aimer's prone position taken out, and the nose rounded off instead. This was rather ugly, but was more streamlined and an improvement. The fat mid-upper turret was taken out altogether, and this again gave less wind resistance. And finally the exhaust stub shrouds were taken off again and the stubs were painted instead with a thick black substance which was impervious to heat, and which did not flake off so hid the red hot glow fairly satisfactorily. All these improvements did make for a better performance, but the real breakthrough came with the Halifax III which came along later with a much improved nose design and more powerful engines, making it a really marvellous aeroplane. But more of that anon.

Operations proceeded whenever the weather permitted, with all the normal trials and tribulations associated with continual flying, but with the occasional comic relief to alleviate the tensions now and again. We also got our third flight, and Squadron Leader Charles Porter was sent in to command it. He was a navigator, and one of the first non-pilots to get an operational command. I had known him previously and was glad to have him with us. He also knew Dinty Moore well, and it helped to make a happy squadron as he was a cheerful and efficient officer. He well deserved the appointment, and went on to finish his second tour of operations with great credit.

I remember a quiet 'Gardening' trip at this time to sow a mine in the sea lane between the Island of Juist and the NW coast of Germany, when the only hostility encountered from the local tribesmen was a long range squirt of heavy tracer hosed up at us from some lonely outpost where the optimistic gunners were only too happy to have something to do during an unexciting vigil. They missed us by miles.

Another memorable flight was a trip to Turin one fine night. I had never been on an Italian target before and thought I would have a look at one since the opportunity presented itself. It was well worth it too. It was a dark but clear night, and crossing the Alps, on the French side we could clearly see the snow-clad peaks below us. Although we were many miles away the massive chunk of Mont Blanc reared up white and menacing, seemingly quite near and towering above us although we were actually flying about 500ft higher than its summit. Even the lower mountain peaks immediately below us looked uncomfortably close.

We dived down to 9,000ft to bomb the Fiat works, and could easily see the dark lanes of streets with the buildings ablaze each side in block after block. I don't remember any flak or not at all the sort of reception we were used to, but we always reckoned that the Italian gunners got to the cellars before the civilian population. Maybe they were elderly third-line troops, or they just didn't have their hearts in the job, but they certainly gave us an easy time. We landed back at Chipping Warden that night, a little short of fuel.

One night at a dusk take-off I was right behind an aircraft which had just started its run, having turned on to the runway as he rolled forward.

As I watched him go he started to swing to starboard. The pilot checked the swing – over-corrected and swung to the left, but a little further than the previous one to the right. I then had to watch fascinated but horrified as he lurched across the runway to starboard again, right on to the grass this time; and then once more to port, with a puff of grey smoke coming from his wheels as the tyres protested violently as the aircraft skidded across the tarmac; then yet again to the right across the runway with the tortured tyres pouring off black smoke this time.

I could hardly bear to look as I fully expected the undercart to collapse under the strain with the inevitable prang followed by fire and explosions. But still watching transfixed, the impossible happened as the pilot yanked the aircraft into the air and staggered off into the dusky sky – at an angle of nearly 90° to the line of take-off. My breath then exploded out of my lungs – I had been holding it sub-consciously all the time – and I heaved a sigh of relief. After a moment to settle myself and the bomb aimer, who had also been utterly fascinated, we took off ourselves – quite straight, I can assure you.

When we arrived back later I went first to the control tower to see who had taken off just before me. They had all been a bit shaken in there too, it seemed. It had been a new crew on their first op with a flight sergeant pilot. I then went down to the crew room for debriefing, and shortly afterwards the crew concerned came in. I laughingly chided the pilot by congratulating him on being the only person ever to have taken off sideways, and told him that we had all had kittens while watching his performance. Also that his Flight Commander must take him up next day to put this fault right and give him the correct drill for checking a swing, before he could do himself, his crew, and his aeroplane a nasty mischief. Happily he and his crew went on to complete a very satisfactory tour of operations, and at one of the worst times of the war as far as bomber losses were concerned. Not very many crews got through a tour in those days.

Another comedy at around this time was played out over the target one night, when a member of a sprog crew enthroned himself on the Elsan chemical closet during the run-up to the target. Whether this need had been brought about by fear or just bad upbringing I never really found out, but while the poor chap was ruminating on the coldness of his cheeks and generally sympathising with the traditional Brass Monkeys, of course the inevitable happened and the aeroplane got caught in the searchlights, with the flak gunners joining in the fun. Normal evasive action would have been more or less all right, but the new pilot started to throw the kite around as if he were handling a fighter, finally attempting to loop the damn thing.

Naturally the aeroplane fell out of the sky as soon as he got it to the vertical, and chummy too fell off the closet with the contents duly spattered all over himself and the inside of the fuselage. The only other people who were not amused – besides the crew themselves that is – were the wretched 'fitters airframe' who had to clear up afterwards.

I had to explain to the crew that it was preferable to arrange these things so as to avoid using the Elsan at all when in the bomber stream, let alone when approaching the target. And I told the pilot that the best way of staying in searchlights was to keep turning in circles or to keep looping if he must, but no one in their right mind would want to try and loop a great bomb-laden Halibag anyway.

Incidentally, the best way of avoiding flak when caught in searchlights and receiving individual attention from the gunners, had by this time been worked out somewhat more mathematically, and since my own rather unfortunate experience in earlier times I had naturally given the matter much thought. But the boffins had now come up with some real technical 'Gen' – RAF term for information. This was that once an aircraft had been coned by searchlights, and

ONLY OWLS AND BLOODY FOOLS FLY AT NIGHT

therefore had its height and course well and truly plotted by the enemy radar, the flak battery crews had to select a shell, set the fuse to the required height. Then from their instruments they had to predict from the speed and course of the aircraft where the shell would have to explode if said aircraft remained on the same heading and height.

All of this might sound as though the bomber had a certain advantage. But not so. We were informed that the whole process from the moment you were spotted, to the explosion of the first burst, took a bare 30 seconds if an aircraft was flying at 18,000ft. So one didn't have any time to loiter. The only answer for a pilot caught in searchlights therefore, was to fly his aeroplane to a point in the sky where the enemy did not expect him to be. In other words to alter course, height, and speed – or a combination of all three – every 30 seconds or less, so that the inevitable crump would go off relatively harmlessly to one side, or above or below. The only snag being that once having been coned by the searchlights, the gunners did not just push up one shell at a time, but started pumping them up by the cartload at any hapless bomber so illuminated, from maybe dozens of guns from the whole area. The pilot would therefore have to go on continually altering course for the duration of his being held in the cone. And it was no good just swinging about wildly, the evasive action had to be strictly controlled so that it took one out of trouble as quickly as possible, so only 20-30° turns were necessarily recommended.

It all sounded very reasonable in theory, and although having some reservations about being dazzled with all this science it was what we were recommending pilots to do for evasive action if they were ever unlucky enough to be caught in this predicament. But we didn't really know if this was 'Pukka Gen' or 'Duff Gen' until I was able to prove the theory quite unintentionally but most conclusively in practice, not very long after, to the whole bomber force one night over Munich.

Amusing things did happen in the air from time to time,

V

even during otherwise dicey situations. One quite frequent occurrence was when damage from enemy fighters or flak would put the hydraulic system out of action, and either cause the undercart to fall down suddenly, or prevent it from being lowered when an aircraft wanted to land back at base. If the wheels fell down while still over enemy territory, it was vital to get them up again as quickly as possible as the drag might prevent the aeroplane from getting back to England at all, because of so much more engine power being necessary to keep the required airspeed. Then the flight engineer would have to try and pump the landing gear up by hand, and if too much hydraulic fluid had been lost it became quite a problem. A reserve supply of fluid was usually carried for emergencies, but this was not enough on some occasions. Furthermore, the undercart would have to be pumped down again manually for the landing.

So it became standard practice to use the coffee ration if this emergency arose. And on the frequent occasions when the coffee had all been used up or had already been consumed, then the alternative emergency drill came into action, which was for the crew to urinate into a container and use that for the hydraulic fluid. The only handy container would invariably be one of the coffee flasks of course, and in spite of the rather dramatic circumstances usually prevailing at those moments, there were some almost hilarious anecdotes of crews trying desperately to squeeze the last ounce of water from among themselves to enable the undercarriage gear to be pumped up or down as the case might be.

One day I was standing on the balcony of our control tower at Snaith with our Station Commander, Group Captain 'Fatty' Gray, watching a number of our aeroplanes taking off and landing on routine practices and air tests, when there was a sudden change of wind direction, and the runway in use had to be switched quickly as there were several aircraft in the circuit buzzing round waiting to land. A smoke candle was being placed outside and about to be lit by the duty controller, this being one way of alerting pilots to a wind change and the CO called out to a young airman standing around outside below us to alter the wind 'T' to the correct direction as well. This was a large white 'T' set outside all control towers as an additional wind direction indicator to pilots and seen clearly from the air. It was sometimes set on rollers for easy movement.

Now this particular airman happened to be one of the crash tender crew who were always standing-by on duty whenever any flying was in progress. He was rather young and very green. He just looked up at the Station Commander and said in rather a pained voice, 'It's not my job, sir.' I saw the back of the CO's neck bulge and rapidly turn bright purple as he exploded into a stream of barrack room invective, which made it quite clear to the unfortunate young Erk that no bloody union rules existed in the RAF and that if he didn't bloody well get on with it he would be up on a bloody charge forthwith! The 'T' was then changed round in record time, and all of us in flying control, as well as the crews of the crash tender and ambulance, were all creased up with suppressed mirth as the CO stumped back inside, his moustache still bristling with rage and indignation.

A most unusual drama took place one evening, although luckily without any fatalities to personnel. The crews had all changed into their flying kit and had just been taken out to their various aircraft to get ready for take-off, and I had just arrived in the control tower as was my habit. After a momentary check of the crew board, I glanced out across the airfield as it was still full daylight, and saw with dismay a tell-tale plume of thick smoke which indicated that something very ominous was happening across the far side. We couldn't see the source because the particular dispersal area was behind a huge mound of earth which formed the gun testing butts, but it was obviously an aeroplane on fire so I had to get out there pretty smartly.

As I tore down the steps to my car, the fire tender had

already started off and I chased it across the grass in my small Hillman. On the other side of the butts there was the horrible sight of one of my beautiful Halibags well and truly alight and burning fiercely. As I left the car and raced up on foot, the fire crew were already playing their chemical hoses on to the fire, but I could see that it was hopeless because underneath the aeroplane were at least three whole containers of incendiaries on the ground – three heaps of brightly burning magnesium.

It was obvious that the petrol tanks were going to go up with a bang very shortly, so I told the aircrew and ground staff to get the hell out of it as they were still standing around dejectedly. There was another Halifax standing nearby, so I nipped smartly in to the driver's seat and with the help of the ground crew started up the two outer engines, then taxied it round behind the butts well away from the burning pyre which would have scattered flaming debris around if the bombs went off. And as I got out of the aeroplane I had just moved, the petrol tanks in the burning aircraft exploded with the characteristic 'Woomph' they made under those circumstances.

The fire tender took five of the aircrew back to the flights while I took the other two, and I was just questioning them on the way across the airfield when we all simultaneously noticed another malevolent plume of smoke coming from a dispersal point almost ahead of us near the control tower.

'Oh, my God, another one', I yelled, and accelerated as fast as possible to the scene of the new crisis, where we found that exactly the same thing had happened there. And again there was absolutely nothing anyone could do.

At this moment a light aeroplane landed and taxied to the control tower, and out stepped the AOC. 'He would arrive for our Bonfire Night Special,' I thought glumly, and went over to meet him.

By this time I had discovered from both bomb aimers concerned that they had simply been doing their normal pre-flight checks at the bomb panel, when some of the incendiary containers had been suddenly deposited on the ground below for no apparent reason. They had of course immediately exploded on contact with the deck, and set off the rest. The whole thing was quite inexplicable.

The AOC was greatly relieved to know that it was 'only' that. He had thought while circling the airfield preparatory to landing that two of our Halifaxes had collided in the air and crashed each side of the airfield with the probable loss of fourteen lives. He said that he would send the accident investigators along next day to sort through the debris and try to find the cause. He then took himself off again while we got the rest of our aircraft off on their mission for that night, leaving the two aeroplanes to burn themselves out – which took quite a while with all that petrol to burn off! A very sad sight.

Even this great drama produced two amusing incidents, the first being when the rear gunner of the second aeroplane to catch fire had been ordered to abandon the aircraft while still firmly earthbound. He swung his turret round and stepped out of the back, saw what was happening, then ran like the clappers out through the main gates and straight up to the village pub – about a mile all told. There, having made the run in record time, he calmed his shattered nerves with copious draughts of the local ale, still clad in full flying kit with the intercom leads of his helmet trailing behind him, and his parachute harness still firmly attached over his thick sheepskin Irvine-Suit.

Pilot Officer 'Donk' Donkersley was an ex-Yorkshire policeman, a tubby chap who was one of the squadron comedians anyway, and quite obviously never at a loss as to the correct action to be taken in any moment of real crisis. The sight of him streaking uphill in full flying gear at a rate of knots was apparently quite something, and which I much regretted having missed myself.

The other laugh we had that night was when one of the fire appliances from the Goole Fire Brigade arrived on the scene.

It had been sent over by their chief to help us when they had seen the two great pillars of smoke, and being only about 5 miles away very nobly decided to lend a hand. Dashing through our main gate to the first blaze they could get to, it did not seem to occur to them as they arrived that our own appliances were not around, and that the group of onlookers standing disconsolately about were only more or less warming their hands at the blaze as it were – albeit at some distance. So they swiftly disembarked, unrolled their hoses, and started to squirt foam onto the blazing entrails when they almost immediately noticed a complete set of very large bombs lying snugly in the middle, cooking nicely and almost incandescent in the white hot centre.

They hadn't said a word to any of us up to this time but were simply going to get on with the job and show us amateurs how it should be done. And again without a word, other than the shout of warning as they saw the deadly heart of the fire, the hoses were suddenly dropped and the crew scrambled hastily aboard their vehicle as one man, and they were off out of it and through the main gate past the guardroom with hoses dragging merrily behind, like some departing wedding chariot. But funnily enough, the bombs in neither fire exploded although having been so thoroughly done to a turn.

The cause of the mishaps turned out to be that these were two brand new aeroplanes which had only just been delivered, and before leaving the factory, there had been some small last minute modification carried out in the nose end. Some brass filings had fallen down unnoticed into the bomb release gear and become embedded in the insulating material between the contact points. These had created a series of 'shorts' throughout the mechanism, making part of the system 'live' when the normal testing was carried out, and activating some of the bomb hooks in the bomb bays. The very same thing had happened at other stations that same evening, when four other Halifaxes were lost as well as our two. What a waste. The Group Captain and I both fervently wished that the AOC would stay away for a few weeks because it seemed that some great drama took place whenever he showed up.

Another somewhat dodgy incident involving a burn-up occurred soon after this when one of our aircraft returning from an operation had a photographic flash bomb hang-up. The pilot reported this over the R/T while he was preparing to land, and that they had not been able to dislodge it. There was nothing very unusual about this, and in itself it was not dangerous. But quite by chance really I had decided to get a breath of fresh air and left Control to go to the dispersal point to see the aircraft in, as it happened to be quite close to the tower. I walked over to where it was still being taxied along the perimeter track, and saw that the pilot had already opened the bomb doors for the armourers to get at the racks when servicing started, as this was the drill. I saw the flash-bomb quite clearly in the pale light of a quarter moon, and noticed in a sort of disinterested way that the small propeller on the nose of the bomb casing was revolving quite rapidly in the breeze. But almost immediately I did a sort of mental double-take as alarm bells jangled in my brain and I realised that another dodgy situation was developing – but fast.

The photo-flash bomb was so designed that as it fell away from the bomb rack with all the other bombs as they were released, a safety pin was automatically withdrawn through being held back by a wire to the rack. This then allowed the small propeller on the nose to rotate freely and unscrew itself in the wind caused by its descent, and when a certain number of turns had been completed, it then fell off completely, allowing a spring to be released. This in turn detonated the flash, all so timed that the flash went off as the rest of the bombs arrived at the ground, and so taking the photograph of each individual's bomb-fall.

On this occasion, the flash-bomb had hung up for some unknown reason. But for some very inexplicable reason the safety pin had fallen out, which was quite another matter. As

V

soon as the pilot opened the bomb doors the detonator propeller had started to unwind as the aircraft was taxied along, and by the time I noticed it was clearly due to fall away and detonate the flash bomb at any moment. And a photo-flash was a lethal weapon in its own night, being packed with magnesium powder which exploded and burnt brightly enough to give full light for a photograph of ground detail to be taken on the darkest night, and it was pretty hot with it!

So I ran out to the front of the aircraft on the pilot's side waving frantically for him to cut the engines, then shouted to him to get his crew out quickly as the flash bomb was 'live'. They needed no second bidding, and we all dived into a nearby slit shelter. We had only just made it when the flash went off with an explosive crack, setting fire immediately to the aeroplane which shortly blew up completely when the petrol tanks exploded moments later. The Halifax was destroyed of course, and ironically the photographic hut was damaged by the blast, but no one was hurt, thankfully.

These few incidents are quoted as examples of the sort of things that were happening throughout the Command at all bomber stations, (and in other operational commands as well probably) on the ground when preparing for any operation or receiving aircraft back from ops. Even with personnel fully trained in the handling, care, and safety regulations concerning all the lethal objects used night after night, catastrophes frequently occurred. They were accepted as occupational hazards, but each time it happened it was a minor nightmare we could well have done without.

It may appear that I am laying it on a bit thick, as the saying goes, but all these things happened inside the four months I was at Snaith. Maybe we were having a run of bad luck, which did happen, and there were other periods at other times when no spectacular excitements took place for several months perhaps. But each station now had eighteen to twenty-four aircraft including reserves, and with most of them being required as frequently as possible, it was really no small wonder that dodgy incidents were always occurring.

While on the subject, two further examples, which happened at other stations, will illustrate how they could, and did, happen anywhere. One was when a Lancaster crashed in 5 Group, loaded with a huge 4,000lb bomb. The Station Commander, Group Captain Gus Walker, was directing rescue operations to free a trapped rear runner when the bomb exploded, killing several nearby and blasting Gus Walker along the runway so that he lost his right arm as a result. He had already completed two tours of operations very successfully as well.

In another Command at Thorney Island, my old Squadron Commander from my Cranwell days, who commanded the station there, Group Captain H.S. Scroggs, was killed when a twin-engined torpedo bomber crashed on take-off one night and burst into flames. Group Captain Scroggs had dashed out to the scene in his car with two or three others and went to look for the crew. As they arrived, the torpedo exploded and they were all killed. The tragic irony of it was that the crew had all got out quickly and were safely out of range of the explosion.

So there were great hazards attending at every airfield whenever aircraft were being prepared for operations. Many members of the crash tender crews received gallantry awards for entering burning aircraft to try and rescue trapped or unconscious crews knowing full well that there would be petrol and sometimes bombs, which might explode at any moment. Our crash tender crews did a magnificent job throughout the war.

One of my Flight Commanders came to me one day to say that one of his new Sergeant Pilots was complaining that he had a 'rogue' aeroplane which in the pilot's opinion was badly warped and difficult to fly straight. It was a new aeroplane, and although this sort of thing had been known, it was so rare that we did not believe it to be possible now. So I asked the Flight Commander if he minded my taking the pilot and crew to flight test the aeroplane concerned, and he readily agreed.

Seated at the controls with the sergeant beside me, we went through the normal pre-flight checks, but in addition I also checked with him all the 'trimmer tab' positions for the adjustment of the control surfaces. We found that both the aileron and rudder trim indicators were several degrees out of the normal central position, and I told him to re-set them back to zero. He looked a bit dubious, but did so. Asked if he knew they were at those settings, he replied that he had adjusted them himself yet still the aircraft would not fly straight.

The 'trimmer tabs' were fixed to the trailing edges of both port and starboard ailerons and rudders. They were small flanges of metal, pivoted or hinged so that they could be moved up and down or from side to side in the case of the rudders, by a mechanical adjuster in the pilot's cockpit for fine tuning of the aircraft 'trim' or attitude. This enabled the pilot to fly more or less 'hands off' the control column or 'feet off' the rudder bar, thus reducing the actual physical effort required for flying an aeroplane for long periods.

So with all trimmers set at neutral, we took off and climbed to 2,000ft where we levelled off. I could not feel any unnatural tendencies to yaw or bank on the way up. So I trimmed the aircraft on the elevator trimming gear (which was a different system for fore and aft trim as it always had to be altered for every landing) so that we were flying absolutely level. Then by very carefully tuning the rudders and aileron trimming tab adjusters, the aeroplane was soon flying absolutely straight and level with hands and feet quite clear of the control column and rudder bar, until an up-current caused a slight bump and I took control again.

Sergeant Cox was watching interestedly, and I changed seats with him, and told him to fly with a minimum of pressure on the controls as well as to take short spells with hands and feet off altogether. He then agreed that it was all right now, and we changed seats again when he checked all the trimmer tab indicators, and found to his astonishment that they were practically central with only very marginal adjustments. The whole crew were all delighted, as were the ground crew who always took things very personally when 'their' aeroplane was criticised.

The very same thing happened again shortly afterwards when a pilot complained that his aircraft could not be climbed to operational heights because it wouldn't fly straight. So we had a full load of dead bombs put on and went through the same performance, only climbing to the necessary height to prove to the crew that there was nothing wrong. In both cases the pilots had adjusted their trimmers in very bumpy conditions, and had over corrected, then gone on with further adjustments which only made matters worse all the time, until the aircraft were crabbing along uncomfortably like some drunk after a heavy night out. Flying an aeroplane trimmed like that would be very tiring, and the two pilots concerned had been – through inexperience only – a little too ham-fisted with the trimmers, when they should have tuned back to zero and started again. So we ended up with a general discussion of the problem with all crews in the crew-room, and everyone checked their trimmers on the very next occasion that they flew.

Now came the night early in March when I was to give an involuntary practical demonstration of correct evasive tactics over a heavily defended target for the benefit of the whole bomber force. An exhibition, I might add, which my crew stated later in no uncertain terms, they would readily have foregone the doubtful pleasure of providing. We had been briefed for a heavy attack on Munich with well over 600 bombers, and I had decided to fly that night because I particularly wanted to get a good aiming point photograph instead of the usual one showing bags of fires and smoke with all ground detail obscured. So I took our bombing leader, Flight Lieutenant McCloy, to try and make certain of this. Flight Lieutenant Bob Parnham, the gunnery leader, came along too for the ride, and to 'get one in'. Flying Officer Harry Keeling, a solid Yorkshire-man, was our navigator. My old faithful Butch Heaton took care of our wireless needs, with Sergeants Steer and Tanner as flight engineer and mid upper gunner respectively.

We set course on a clear but very dark night which necessitated a fair amount of instrument flying since it was a deep penetration and which was quite enjoyable. We flew a little faster than the flight plan indicated, as we wanted to get our bombing done and a good photograph taken very early on in the attack, before too much smoke obliterated the ground, and therefore we planned to bomb immediately after the first Pathfinder Marker Flare hit the ground.

The flight out was uneventful, and I think that the route planned and the feint attacks laid on for that night must have proved very successful because I cannot remember having seen any night fighter combats, and although the main force was behind us, Bob Parnham did not report any from the rear turret position either. I do remember flying along someone else's vapour trail and calling to the two gunners to keep an extra sharp eye open for fighters, who would naturally follow con-trails if they happened to pick one up. Also, on the last leg into Munich while running up on a north-easterly course, we saw far below us a tiny square of electric lighting which probably indicated the position of a POW camp. I told the navigator to plot it as accurately as possible, and couldn't help thinking how it would cheer up the inmates to hear the steady roar of several hundred bombers droning high over their heads on their way to knock hell out of some enemy town.

As we came up to ETA target, I selected the lever to open the bomb doors, and called the bomb aimer to let him know that we were all set. McCloy had been down in the nose for some time getting everything ready himself, but the ground and sky ahead was unnaturally quiet and dark still, with no searchlights or flak. I was just asking the navigator if he was sure we were on track, when the first red marker went down bang on the dot, and almost dead ahead, making a vivid splash of colour on the ground. A splendid piece of navigating on Keeling's part. A slight pressure on the rudder bar was all that was required to point the nose directly at the ground marker for the bomb aimer to line up his sights.

At that moment, the first searchlight flicked on, and absolutely smack on us without any searching around. It had a mauve tinge to it, and was obviously a master beam controlled by radar which had nailed us so accurately. For the second it found us, every single searchlight in the whole area was switched on immediately and fastened on us, some eighty beams counted by the rear gunner all pointing at us personally. It was incredible, and so fast. And of course we all knew that the flak would start coming up at us at any second. And it did. By the ton.

I couldn't turn round and make a second run in because the searchlights wouldn't let go of us now anyway, and with the rest of the bomber force piling in behind I could not fly against the stream and risk a collision. So we just had to plough through it all and get on with it. I told McCloy that I would be taking evasive action, but would try and aim on average for the target marker, and that he was to direct me on to it at the last moment.

All this took only seconds of course, but the flak was already coming up non-stop, and so thick that you could almost get out and walk on it, to quote some joker who once used that phrase in a report. I had turned 30° to starboard the moment the mauve searchlight had got us, and lost about 300ft of height in the first twenty-five seconds. My head was down on my chest, partly to avoid being blinded by the glare of the searchlights, and partly because I was concentrating furiously on the instruments in a grim effort to keep to the calculated set pattern of evasive tactics called for in this situation as explained earlier. Then came a 40° turn to port and losing another 200 or 300ft in the next twenty-five seconds. Again another 20° to the right to get somewhere near the marker, but this time using our extra speed gained in the recent dives to gain 300ft or so in order to confound the radar trackers even more, and counting the seconds off in my head.

A sudden yell from McCloy: 'Left – left, Skipper, steady' and an agony of suspense before he called the welcome 'Bombs gone', and the aircraft lifted as the sudden release of the heavy load freed it from the extra weight. Harry Keeling was standing beside me I noticed now but had not seen him arrive.

Closing the bomb doors I altered course again to port, diving more steeply to speed our departure. The flak continued to thump around us, like the usual giant hand banging on the side of the fuselage. We kept flying through clumps of smoke, the smell of burnt cordite penetrating inside the aeroplane and adding to the drama. Starboard – port – starboard – port and so on, dive, dive, climb, dive – losing more height than climbing, in order to keep a higher speed to escape from the torment. The whole crew were absolutely silent. Not a sound from anyone when normally a few comments are made over a target, even if only to report an aircraft shot down, just a tense unnatural silence.

The crumping and dazzle continued until we had traversed the whole area and had started to leave the town behind us, when as suddenly as it had begun all the searchlights and guns deserted us to return to the skies above the battered city. Even now, the crew who had been absolutely transfixed by the sight and implications of what we had just been through, still had nothing to say as we were left alone in the darkness, our night vision up the spout and not really yet believing our luck. I suddenly realised that I was sweating as if I was in a Turkish bath, and it was not just from physical exertion! My mouth was as dry as the proverbial acrobat's jock strap. We had started our bombing run at 18,000ft, and in the process of our evasive action we had come out on the other side at 14,000ft. But we had come out, that was the thing.

As my night vision gradually returned to normal, I asked the navigator for the exact course home, on to which I had already turned roughly. He was now back at his table and gave me the exact course. I told the engineer to get a flask of coffee out so that we could have a little each, but no relaxing because we were still in the danger zone from fighters. But the tension had relaxed.

'Ye Gods, Skipper, that was quite something,' said McCloy.

'Do you know how long we were in that cone and being shot at?' asked Harry Keeling.

I said that I really hadn't had the time to notice.

'Eight minutes,' he said.

'It seemed more like eight bloody hours,' I answered with feeling. 'Now settle down, chaps, and let's concentrate on getting home.'

We had a trouble-free run across the Continent, and once over the North Sea the sandwiches were brought out and we finished off our coffee. A picnic never tasted so good. Only strictly official business was discussed over the inter-com from then on, as we were all still unwinding and too occupied with our own thoughts for unnecessary chatter.

On getting out of our aircraft at dispersal and preparing to get into the crew bus, one of the sergeants in my crew put his hand on my arm and said quite quietly and simply, 'Thanks, Skipper.' I looked at him but couldn't say anything, and only patted him on the shoulder. Just at that moment I felt quite moved, and for a fleeting second somehow indestructible, as if I were certain that nothing worse could happen to me now. Damned silly of course, but delayed shock or delayed relief or whatever, had taken over for a few moments.

There was always a tremendous feeling of elation or euphoria as you stepped on to the ground after a long flight, or after any operation for that matter, and which kept up in the debriefing room amid all the banter and excitement of getting back.

The crew room was buzzing more loudly than usual as I went in with my crew. One of our pilots, Flight Lieutenant Ron Hay, who seemed to specialise in getting home first by cutting corners and flying faster than he should, against all the rules of course, called out as we entered, 'Hullo, sir, did you see that great stupid twat who went over the target at the beginning and took all the flak and searchlights with him?'

I replied, 'Hay, consider yourself on a charge for insubordination for calling your CO by vulgar names.'

'Good God, was it you?' he said. 'Then thanks very much, sir. I followed through just behind you and had the jammiest trip ever!' And several other pilots and crews said the same.

In fact for eight minutes we had given a great number of our bomber crews a free run over the target for a change, and I am sure they were duly grateful.

Harry Keeling said that when he came forward to stand beside me over the target, he could see even in spite of my oxygen mask, that I looked absolutely grim-faced, and added that all the crew had their parachutes already clipped to their harnesses from the moment the flak started 'just in case' of a sudden need to bale out, which they had definitely expected. But the coveted aiming-point photograph was denied us because the print was completely white and blank – a slight case of over-exposure! And the ultimate insult came when we all went out to the aeroplane next morning to count the holes, only to find that there was not one single scratch to show for our ordeal.

A couple of weeks later I decided to take the bombing leader again to try and get a clear photograph of an aiming point, because there was to be an experiment with the target marking technique. The target was the U-boat pens at St Nazaire on the French Atlantic coast, which had to be attacked with 2,000lb armour piercing bombs in order to penetrate the thick reinforced concrete constructions which formed the casements under which the U-boats were housed, and only a few incendiaries were carried to set fire to the dock installations.

Some clever boffin had dreamed up the idea of laying the Pathfinder target markers at a distance from the actual target, and the bomb aimers would have to 'aim-off' 3in to one side of the coloured flares burning on the ground, where the concrete pens would then receive the bombs – hopefully. How the C-in-C ever got himself talked into this one we shall never know, but we all thought the idea a bit crazy. It had something to do with trying to minimise damage to the rest of this French town, I believe, most laudable in itself but we could not quite understand how it would work in practice, because bomb aimers would all have a different idea of how to measure the 3in, and from what datum point etc. And these doubts turned out to be completely justified when the photographic analysis of the raid was made later.

However, we had the usual fairly peaceful trip out and the only excitement was when I saw a Lancaster suddenly sweep straight across our bows at about 100 yards range as we were on our run in towards the target. This was not even considered a near miss in those days of course. So I gave McCloy a nice steady bombing run to give him bags of time to line up and get a good aim, continuing straight on after the 'bombs gone' so that our bomb bursts would show up bang in the middle too.

On the way home, with St Nazaire now well behind us, we saw a succession of double-red Very cartridges being fired off way down below us on the same track that we were making, and keeping pace with us just ahead. It was a dark night, but clear, and I had started to lose height to go and investigate if someone was in trouble, and perhaps escort them home if we could find them in the darkness, when the pyrotechnic display ended, and so did our chance of finding the aircraft.

It was not until we returned to base that we had any worries at all, that night, because although we could see our beacon, there was no sign of the circuit lights or runways as a thick ground fog had developed just before our ETA, so we had to circle the beacon and await diversion instructions. The duty controller soon came up with orders for us to proceed to Nutts Corner, but none of us had ever heard of it before, and it was not on the navigator's 'gen-sheet'. So having asked where the hell it was, and being informed that it was a new station in Northern Ireland, I asked the controller to try Group again for somewhere a bit nearer, as I didn't fancy stooging all that way for breakfast. But all stations in Yorkshire and East Anglia were closing in apparently, and although most aircraft had been got down safely before it became too thick, there were still a few floating around with no homes to go to – like ourselves.

However, it turned out that after all it was still reasonably clear at Pocklington in our own group, it being on slightly higher ground, and we were sent there, only a few minutes away. I called up on R/T as we arrived at their beacon, and was told to orbit at 2,000ft, which indicated that there were probably three or four other aircraft in the circuit below me, so I started to circle the airfield lights to wait for further instructions. But suddenly, and quite unexpectedly our call sign and letter came up over the R/T, giving us permission to land.

At that precise moment I was still at 2,000ft and in the down-wind quarter of the circuit, and strictly speaking should have gone round again to lose 1,000ft of excess height. But with the fog closing in rapidly I was not going to waste any time. So I dropped the undercart, put on half flap, and throttled right back to a fast tick-over all in one quick motion, and making the aircraft sink like the proverbial brick at a rate of descent that would have shaken the purists rigid. Arriving in a matter of moments at the correct height of about 400ft, at the mouth of the 'funnel', I slapped on full flap, opened the throttles a bit for more engine power, then touched down to a perfect three point 'arrival' to round off a most unusual and speedy approach, with which I was extremely pleased but kept rather quiet about as it was not the sort of example to set for the inexperienced to try and emulate. But I had a good excuse, for by the time we had been directed to dispersal and disembarked into the crew bus, the airfield was completely closed by fog.

Incidentally we did get a perfect photograph too, showing our stick of bombs bursting quite clearly – right in the middle of the French countryside on the outskirts of St Nazaire, where only the local livestock had been disturbed. Many other photographs taken that night showed open fields or the outside edge of the town. So much for 'aiming off', a technique which was thankfully never used again.

The CO at Pocklington, whom I knew slightly, offered me a bed in his own quarters, but I declined because I had made it a matter of personal policy to sleep with the rest of my crew in the 'diversion hut' whenever we had been ordered to land away from base after operations. Every station had to keep twenty or thirty beds available for possible diversions, and I saw no reason to be separated from my crew until we had returned safely to our own base. We had all been 'dicing' together in the same aeroplane, so why shouldn't we share the same diversion dormitory for one night? The junior officers had no option on these occasions, so I did the same for morale purposes.

A really incredible accident happened one night to one of my crews returning from operations. We had the usual one or two missing crews that night, and had gone to bed after debriefing and breakfast. Getting up later that morning, I made the inevitable first call to flying control to study the day's weather charts, and had not been there long before an outside telephone call was put through to me. It came from the wilds of Yorkshire and was the sergeant pilot of one of our 'missing' aircraft of the night before, reporting in and asking for transport to bring himself and five other members of his crew back to the station. The seventh member – the wireless operator – had unfortunately been killed in the crash. We sent out for them, and also to collect the guns, ammunition, and other valuable removable items of equipment from the crashed aeroplane.

It transpired that they had passed their ETA base without having seen any aerodrome beacons at all, and were flying around in cloud trying to get a W/T fix. They were at 3,000ft according to their altimeter, which they reckoned to be a reasonably safe height, when they suddenly felt and heard a tremendous bang on the underside of the fuselage, and naturally thought that they had been in a collision with another aircraft. There was so much vibration that the pilot had to throttle right back, and before he could order the crew to bale out there were more grinding and crunching noises from underneath him, and a very marked deceleration indicated to him that they were probably on the ground, however fantastic that may have seemed. So he switched off the engines and let nature take its course.

The aircraft continued in a splintering nose down slither until it finally came to rest, and on scrambling hurriedly out the crew found that they were on a heather-covered mountainside with the belly of the aeroplane ripped to pieces and the airscrews all bent backwards at 90°. Only the poor wireless operator had been killed because his working station was down in the nose right underneath the pilot's feet, and just at the point where the fuselage had struck the ground. He would have been killed instantly, but another foot higher and they would have got away with it, although another foot lower would have resulted in the whole crew being killed because an almost head-on collision with a mountain at 180mph would have meant a complete wrap-up.

They had just grazed the top of a mountain in the Pennines and juddered on to a stop in the rough ground and heather. They sheltered in the body of the fuselage for the rest of the night, since the aeroplane was more or less in one piece, and at daylight had moved off downhill to find a village from where they could telephone for help. Just another of the typical lucky escape stories with which the annals of the RAF in general, and of Bomber Command in particular, are crammed.

One of my Flight Commanders came to me one day after we had been warned for an operation night and the crew lists had been issued, but well before briefing so the target was not known outside the operations room. One of his air gunners had told him that he refused to fly that night, or ever again in fact. I told him to bring the sergeant gunner to me, and he repeated to us both that he would not fly again. Asked why, he stated that he could not face it any more (having done only three or four sorties) that he had a wife and child and could not go on.

I told him that I also had a wife and two children, that thousands of other men in all three services had families, and that we all had to carry on. Did he want others to do his fighting for him?

How would he feel when his family and friends found out that he had been too yellow, and left others to do the dirty work? And did he know that he would be put into the army and given a rifle to go and face the enemy that way? And so on. I wasn't too sure of that last ploy, but he said that he would prefer that, but would not fly again. I then told him that if he did not turn up for briefing he would be arrested and put in the guard-room overnight.

The Flight Commander then had to get a stand-by gunner to take the man's place as we both knew that he would not attend, and the station warrant officer was also alerted to go and fetch the sergeant from his billet when the time came. This duly happened, and the wretched NCO was taken in after packing his kit, and incarcerated in the guard-room cell for the night before being whisked away to Group HQ next morning.

Neither as a Flight Commander nor Squadron Commander in my previous squadrons had I come across this before, but everyone was aware that it happened from time to time throughout the Command. Later on when I commanded stations for nearly two years, I can only recollect one other case. There were occasional reports of some squadron or other having minor epidemics of such refusals, or more usually the other manifestation of loss of morale, through a spate of 'early returns', when pilots made weak excuses for abandoning an operational sortie when approaching the enemy coast. These were nearly always the result of poor leadership, and a quick change of Squadron or Flight Commanders – or both – plus the splitting up of the offending crews for further training, was usually enough to get a squadron back on an even keel again.

The incidence of refusals to fly was really quite low under the circumstances, and surprisingly few men went 'LMF', as it was termed officially – 'Lack of Moral Fibre'. At one time I believe that they were sent into the army or reduced to the lowest rank in the RAF for the more menial duties, but we never quite knew what happened. In the later stages of the war, the 'Trick Cyclists' (psychiatrists) used to get hold of them, and we rather got the feeling that they would try and dig out psychiatric reasons and excuses for them. But those who mastered their fears and 'pressed on regardless' as we put it, were more than scathing at this approach and naturally resented it strongly.

Everyone who flew on operations had their moments of doubt and fear, although it was very seldom – if ever – expressed openly, and it just had to be conquered, jokes about 'dicing with death', 'going for a Burton', 'due for the chop' and so on, were the only open admission of those private thoughts, and of course it was always going to happen to someone else and never to themselves personally.

I don't mind admitting now that I certainly had the odd moment of doubt during my second tour, when in the small hours I would very occasionally be unable to sleep and lay wishing I could break a leg or catch pneumonia and get away from it all with a cast-iron excuse. It would not have been human to have felt otherwise, and I know that others must have felt the same judging from the look of strain on some faces when chaps were halfway through a tour and the odds against survival had shortened to nil. But in the morning light it was all over, and mixing with the others, going about our daily business, and above all knowing that an example had to be set, one forgot the previous night's misgivings.

Squadron and Flight Commanders just had to be that much more openly cheerful and seemingly unconcerned in order to get the best from their crews. There were some who had the reputation of being 'flak happy' and fearless, like Leonard Cheshire, Charles Pickard, Guy Gibson, Willy Tait, Pat Daniels, Harik Iveson, Jock Calder, and many others who just went on and on, eventually clocking up about 100 operations against all the odds, until they were finally taken off flying, or the war ended, or they were killed. These – and many others – were all exceptionally brave men, and to be that they must have had their own fears at times. To my knowledge one of them was a bundle of nerves at one stage, and yet they continued with the full knowledge that they were living on borrowed time anyway. In some strange way, the urge to go on flying operationally was a kind of drug which forced many to press on when they could have stood down with honour.

I think that the one moment when one's stomach did turn over sometimes, was when everyone had got settled in for the briefing, and the curtain over the wall map was pulled dramatically aside to reveal the target for the night. When it was one of the well-known hot spots, and the route marked out showed areas of defence which had to be flown over or near, then a groan would, go up from the assembled crews, followed by a sick feeling in the pit of the stomach. It would quickly fade as briefing progressed; then having a meal, getting dressed in flying gear and so on occupied our time and put other thoughts out of our minds. Once in our aircraft too, getting ready for take-off, climbing on the way to the target, occupied with the business of flying, each member of the crew with their own particular duties to carry out, and looking out for other aircraft there was no time to worry about other things. That is, until one saw the barrage over the target from a distance and knew that you had got to plough through it. If attacked by a night fighter, or got coned, or were shot at personally by flak, then one's fears were translated into action for self-preservation and the necessity to evade the immediate danger, and were quite different to the sort of apprehension which occasionally took over in the still hours of the night.

Then the excitement was almost exhilarating in a peculiar way, even though the circumstances were frightening and deadly.

As against that, the tremendous feeling of relief, satisfaction, and sense of achievement which overtook you as your aircraft touched down and you rumbled to dispersals, cannot be clearly described as it was an experience on its own. The warmth and comradeship of the debriefing session, with a cup of hot coffee sometimes laced with rum in cold weather; the good-humoured banter and line-shooting as we all settled down together in the mess hall for our operational breakfast of bacon and eggs; then going to bed with tensions unwound and thankful at having come through another trip, all created that marvellous atmosphere which normally prevailed at bomber stations, and was so unforgettable by those lucky enough to have experienced it.

Perhaps this was why those spontaneous parties would erupt sometimes when the 'ops scrubbed' came through at the last moment, the late cancellation prohibiting a visit to the nearest town. Then large quantities of weak wartime brew would he consumed to the accompaniment of bawdy barrack-room songs, or noisy and childish games in a mad rough and tumble of debagging, muffin-man, sooty footprints on the ceiling, spilled beer, high-cockalorum, and all the other variations including Cardinal Puff – a safety valve perhaps at the sudden release of tension and the knowledge that all was well for another day or two anyway.

Everyone got particular enjoyment from those impromptu thrashes in the mess, and once again they were a real morale builder with all joining in the fun from the Station Commander down. I well remember an amusing by-product of ours at Snaith, when it was noticed by some that Squadron Leader Charlie Porter seemed to be able to hold his beer much longer than anyone else before he went off for relief, and this reputation very quickly produced some humorist who started a sweepstake whenever one of these parties got under way as to the precise time when Charlie would have to go. Of course he soon twigged as to what was going on because a great cheer would go up as he left the bar. And, from then on he used to become absolutely cross-legged trying to hold on and pretending not to know what was going on, before he dashed out to avoid disaster. We would all be hooting with laughter, looking at our watches, and urging him to leave or hang on longer for a record according to each individual's estimate for that evening.

On another occasion during one of these binges, I organised a moustache-growing contest, and if anyone had already started they were ceremoniously dry-shaved so that all would start equal. Some wanted me to participate and get shaven, but as organiser I took the coward's way out and said that I would be the judge. I had always had a moustache since being 18½ years old, and look completely naked without one. But I agreed not to trim it while the competition was in progress. And although the contestants were gradually reduced in numbers unfortunately, a couple of really good sets of whiskers were achieved in the allotted time, and my own reached 'Whacko' proportions, spreading from ear to ear. All very childish it may seem to some, but nevertheless all part of the need for keeping up a good squadron spirit and high morale. It is frequently 'the little things in life wot counts', as the Bishop was once reputed to have said somewhere, I believe.

These were not drunken orgies, in case anyone is getting the wrong impression. Wartime beer was very weak, and filled the belly rather than going to the head. But a few beers in a very cheerful atmosphere was all that transpired, and the boisterousness was all part of being among friends and enjoying a few hours of real relaxation.

When a stand-down was given early, or the squadron was not put on the battle order for a night, an aircrew bus would be authorised to take all those wanting to go into the nearest town for a visit to the squadron's favourite pub, or to a local hop for a few beers and a bit of crumpet – usually in that order of preference – as there were always many willing young ladies only too happy to help these young and cheerful aircrews to enjoy life to the full while they had the opportunity. And who can blame them? They had no future to look forward to, and therefore just lived for the day.

Some would go quietly to a bedsitter or digs where a wife would be waiting unofficially and patiently for a husband who might never turn up again. Others would take the opportunity to have an early night after a few quiet beers in the mess. There were all sorts, mostly from nineteen years old to their early twenties, a few in their late twenties or sometimes even over thirty. They came from all walks of life, the serious-minded, the flippant, the brash or raucous. At times they appeared undisciplined by some standards, but on duty in the air all were members of a team and as one in their application and dedication to the job which had to be done, proud of their contribution to the war and the Command in which they served.

At the end of March, Berlin was suddenly laid on for attention after it had been left alone for a while, so I thought that a personal appearance was indicated to show willing, and to leave my visiting cards for the third time on that psychologically important recipient of the Command's attention. At briefing the usual groan and buzz of excitement went up at the unveiling ceremony. We all knew that it was a long haul in and out, heavily defended when you got there, with the route unavoidably passing close to other strongly defended areas, and a long drag over enemy territory both ways to give the night fighters plenty of time to practise their interceptions. Dummy feint attacks were part of the night's plan as usual, and we all hoped fervently that they would fool the Luftwaffe for part of the time at least, as they frequently did.

Butch Heaton, who was now acting as Signals Leader, and was as usual coming with me that night, caused much hilarity when he started his signals briefing immediately after the intelligence officer's opening, by saying something about, 'This is a piece of cake tonight, chaps, after all the Wingco's going!' It sounded as though I only picked the easy ones, and this tonight was as simple as a trip to Margate on a Saturday afternoon. But he produced a roar of laughter, and the tension relaxed immediately.

When my turn came to finalise the session, I made a suitable remark to Butch thanking him for his confidence or something similar, but because of his chance remark the whole atmosphere had been much less tense than would normally have been the case with this target.

All went well for us personally, and we had a clear run both ways, and it seemed to have been a successful raid. The flak over the Big City was its usual heavy concentration, with quite a number of the new 'frightener' recently observed being used. These were thought by some to be trying to simulate an exploding bomber, and consequently came to be known generally as a 'Scarecrow' burst. But to me it looked absolutely like a huge chrysanthemum appearing in a white burst for a couple of seconds, and similar to some of the colourful bursts now seen in firework displays on major occasions. Only I thought that the flaming petals were phosphorus shrapnel designed to burst downwards on top of aircraft as opposed to the more normal upward moving shrapnel. Ron Flay thought the same, and much to the amusement of everyone else, used to put his tin hat on over his flying helmet when running over the target.

In mid-April a long range operation wag ordered for an attack on Pilsen in Western Czechoslovakia, with the Skoda works the object of our attention. It was the deepest penetration yet, and a gasp of surprise went up when the crews saw it. The route was good from the point of view of defences, and not much was expected from the target area either judging from reconnaissance photographs. It was a huge factory complex making heavy guns and tanks, and had never been visited before. The diversions had been well planned too. Bombing was to be from between 4 and 6,000ft, and the weather report was fair. The general feeling was that this would be a reasonable trip, if rather long.

We had eighteen aircraft flying that night, and as the first crews arrived back after a $10^{1/2}$ hour flight, it became apparent that things had not gone at all well from the weather and navigational aspect. There was a lot more cloud over Eastern Germany than forecast, which made for great difficulty in finding the target. 'Gee' would not work at that range, and the Pathfinder markers were scattered too as they had found difficulties with their beam marking apparatus too. As expected, there was little or no trouble from ground defences, but a very scattered raid resulted.

Furthermore, Dinty Moore – a very experienced pilot and a Flight Commander – reported that many crews disobeyed the flight plan ordered, and bombed from much higher altitudes because so many photo-flashes were going off way above him while he was flying at 4,000ft over the target area himself. There was no excuse for this because of the few defences, although it may have been that cloud had made them decide to go higher. So I was very shaken when no fewer than five of my crews failed to return that night. We put it down to the fact that my chaps had fully obeyed instructions, and had spent time in searching for the target, or had run into a defended zone on the way out or back. Losses in the Command generally that night were not unduly high. But we had virtually lost a whole flight. Such was the luck of the draw.

About three or four months later, however, Warrant Officer McCrea who was pilot of one of our missing aircraft that night arrived back in England having avoided capture after being shot down and then found his way back with the help of the underground. A very fine effort. I was away from the squadron by the time he arrived back though. I also learned after the war when I met him accidentally, that the navigator, Flying Officer Graham Spencer, had also had a go at getting home, and had been at large for over a week before being captured. Unfortunately for him he was captured by the Gestapo and not by the police or Wehrmacht, and received some very rough treatment before they handed him over to the Luftwaffe to be taken to one of their POW camps. He had made a very gallant effort to evade capture and get home.

A few days after this another long range attack was ordered to Stettin on the Baltic coast, and I decided to go myself as I had missed the Pilsen raid. The flight plan for this attack was most unusual, in that we were briefed to fly right across the North Sea and Denmark at no higher than 400ft. It was a full moon night with a brilliant clear weather forecast. Normally Command avoided deep penetrations at the full moon period because losses on such occasions had proved too heavy to bear. However it was hoped that by keeping low down under the enemy radar scanners, with a spoof attack in another area altogether, the night fighters might be led off elsewhere to leave the main attack comparatively unmolested. So this plan had been devised to keep the enemy guessing as to the direction of attack, and a lower than average loss rate resulted in spite of the ideal conditions for night fighter interceptions.

After crossing Denmark virtually at nought feet, we then had to turn south-east for the leg to Stettin, and climb to bombing height on that course, and that is where it was hoped that the fighters would have been seduced away from by the feint attack down south.

Of course the major problem was that 500 or more bombers crossing the North Sea and Denmark twice – both out and back – all at under 400ft was itself going to be a bit dodgy, but it was expected that the full moon would give enough light to allow us to see each other far enough away to prevent collisions. In the event it turned out, for most crews, to be a marvellously impressive, and even enjoyable trip. Flying for hours at 400ft over the sea required much more than normal concentration by the pilots, and the gunners, bomb aimers, and flight engineers had to keep a continual

V

and careful look-out for other aircraft, as well as the pilots too. But the very bright light of the full moon helped enormously, and in fact we ourselves saw no other aeroplane near us on the way out.

Approaching the Danish coast the occasional burst of tracer was squirted up from the odd flak-ship or shore battery. But no casualties were caused that we saw, although in other areas a few aircraft throughout the Command were reported as having been caught in this fashion, and at those low altitudes there was little chance of getting away with even minor damage if a flak gunner was at all accurate.

Then we went down to 150ft at the Danish coast for the sheer fun of low flying – and for safety as well – the countryside being bathed in a brilliant silver light almost as clear as daylight. Screaming over the fields at 180mph and passing groups of houses, where we saw lights go on in upstairs windows and people leaning out of the yellow squares waving madly to us and obviously cheering us on our way, which in itself gave us great satisfaction. We raced over a huge circle of red lights which denoted an airfield, but we were too quickly past it and too low for the gunners to get a crack at anything. Suddenly there was a huge explosion only half a mile ahead, where one of our bombers had flown smack into a windmill on top of a slight mound – I witnessed the whole calamity – and we nosed up to fly past seconds later, looking sadly at the burning debris and wondering who had misjudged his height so tragically.

Out over the Baltic, we turned south-east on the last long leg, climbing steadily towards Stettin which was already burning fiercely as we arrived, with smoke belching up to 10,000ft or more. There was all the appearance of a very concentrated and successful attack, and the defences were either weaker than usual, or had been overwhelmed by the sheer weight and concentration of aircraft. Then after our run over the target, we turned north-west again in a shallow dive down to sea level for the homeward journey.

At about 8,000ft on the way down I saw a single-seater Focke Wulf 190 suddenly shoot across our nose only about 50 yards ahead. It was in a steep turn on its starboard wing-tip and in plain view to us, seemingly trying to get round behind us. But I wasn't having any and dived steeply to port, away from the moonlight, weaved gently for a spell to make sure it wasn't following and the gunners saw no more of it. Then we went back on a westerly course and right down on the deck again over Denmark without further incident.

As we crossed the Danish coast and went out over the North Sea on the homeward stretch, flying at 400ft once more, I noticed a Stirling bomber on my starboard side at the same height and about 150 yards away. I expect he saw me too, for we kept each other company right across the sea until we approached the English coast and we climbed to 2,000ft towards Yorkshire, and he slid underneath us to port, heading for East Anglia. The squadron had no losses that night, and the Command as a whole lost well below the average. For us, this helped to make up for our Pilsen losses which were soon put at the back of our memories. We could never afford to dwell on 'Bad Nights', or on losing friends, as those things just had to be set aside mentally and as quickly as possible.

At the end of April the AOC came round again, but this time during the afternoon. He asked me to drive him round the dispersal points where the ground crews were preparing our aircraft for the night's operation, so that he could speak to them all in turn for a few moments while they were working.

I noticed also that he seemed to be questioning me rather closely on my time in 4 Group and on my operational experience generally. He had been AOC when I was in 76 and 78 Squadrons previously, as he had taken over the group from 'Maori' Cunningham in about March 1941. Also I had been his Wing Commander Ops at Group HQ for a few months in 1942. I had also known him pre-war during my Fleet Air Arm period when he was Wing Commander Flying on the *Furious*, so I just thought that this was his way of showing a personal interest in my doings. But on 2nd May he telephoned to tell me to go over to RAF Station, Burn – which was a satellite to Snaith at that time, and only recently opened – to take over as their first Station Commander with the acting rank of Group Captain to match the job. I had to go over right away, after having the extra ring sewn on to my tunic by the camp tailor.

During our telephone conversation I asked the AOC whether he expected Station Commanders to fly on operations occasionally, and he replied, 'Not in your case. I want experienced Station Commanders who have done operational tours, and I also want to keep them.'

This was a sound policy adopted throughout the Command, because having to brief the chaps night after night for the dangerous work involved, and living among them in close contact, they needed to know that their immediate Senior Commander was not asking them to do things he had not done himself – and was still prepared to do if necessary. On the other hand, new Station Commanders who had not done any bomber operations were expected to 'get some in' for those very reasons. And most of them did of course. If they didn't they were soon posted away.

CHAPTER SIX

Station Commander

A T Burn, No 431 Squadron was operating with Wellington III's powered by Bristol radial engines. They were very good aircraft, and the crews liked them. From the moment I arrived operations proceeded as normally whenever the squadron was called, and which naturally was whenever the group operated. And very soon there occurred the most splendid example of courage, initiative and devotion to duty which it was my privilege to have been concerned with at any time under my command, both up until then or in the future.

A new Flight Lieutenant pilot was posted to 431 Squadron at about the same time as I arrived at Burn. He had completed one tour of operations and was now starting his second, and had done only one sortie when detailed for this particular night. He took a very young sergeant bomb aimer – Sergeant Sloan – a flying officer navigator, and two more sergeants for wireless operator and rear gunner. Over the target in the Ruhr, and almost immediately after dropping the bombs, there was a sudden burst of flak right under the tail unit which blasted the aircraft into a vertical dive.

Thinking that the tail had been blown off, the pilot ordered the crew to bale out and let himself out of the top hatch. The rear gunner escaped too by rotating his turret and falling out backwards in the approved style. Meanwhile the Wellington quickly accelerated into a screaming dive which prevented the others from getting out because of the wind speed over the escape hatches. Sergeant Sloan had been thrown into the nose of the aircraft by the sudden dive, but after a frenzied and difficult scramble uphill, managed to scrape into the pilot's seat. There he tried to heave back on the control column to level the aeroplane off and slow the speed down sufficiently to allow the three remaining to get out of the crippled Wellington. He had closed the throttles, but the control

172

surfaces were absolutely rigid with the speed of the dive as the aircraft was still going like the clappers almost vertically downhill. It was only when both the navigator and wireless operator dropped into the nose and pushed on the control column from the front, that between them the 'Wimpy' was gradually eased out of its terrifying downward plunge and got on an even keel once more without pulling the wings off.

In fact Sloan used the excess speed to re-gain some of the height which had been lost, because now that they had slowed down, he discovered that the controls seemed to be functioning more or less normally. It must be explained now that this boy Sloan, who had not yet celebrated his nineteenth birthday, had always shown a great interest in piloting since he first started training as a bomb aimer, and at every opportunity had found his way into the link trainer hut and persuaded the instructors to give him some tuition. His own pilot also had encouraged him by allowing him to sit at the controls during practice flights, to fly straight courses under his close supervision, so he did know how to keep a course and make gentle turns.

All this was now going to pay off, because feeling that the aeroplane was flyable, Sloan asked the navigator for a course for home. He intended to have a bash at getting back to England, at the same time telling the other two that they could bale out then and there if they wished, but adding that he was going to bale out when he got back over England. Those two stalwarts told him in no uncertain terms that if he was going to try and get back, then they were jolly well coming with him. So they set course, climbing again to gain more height.

The starboard engine was beginning to run roughly and vibrate, so Sloan throttled it back to preserve some power for as long as possible, and pressed calmly on towards the enemy coast. They got into some trouble for a few minutes when flying over a defended area, and had to take evasive action to avoid searchlights and flak, but this was successfully negotiated and they soon crossed the Dutch coast and were out over the North Sea without further interference. But the starboard engine rapidly deteriorated until it was running so roughly and hot that fire threatened, and Sloan had to switch it off altogether, feathered the airscrew and continued on the one engine until they reached the English coast at Suffolk, well on course.

By this time the port engine also was showing signs of trouble, so the pilot asked the others to bale out while he would try and get the aircraft down at some flare-path or other – preferably back at base but sooner if necessary. The visibility was good, and there were many airfields *en-route* which would be lit up, but his partners in this epic were by now so confident in their pilot, that they said they would stick with him as he might need some help with the landing, undercart and flaps etc.

So they pressed on for Burn. The port engine began to get extremely dodgy and Sloan very sensibly decided to lob down at the next flare-path they saw, and which showed up quite soon. Getting permission to land by Aldis Lamp signal, they came in to make a perfect approach and landing. The only sign of the pilot's inexperience was that towards the end of the landing run, and because there was only one engine running, the aircraft did what is known as a 'Ground Loop', that is, it lurched off to starboard against the 'dead' engine and did a complete tight circle out of control on the ground, before coming to rest. This usually resulted in a burst tyre at the least, or even a collapsed undercart, but Sloan had kept the aircraft straight long enough for it to have slowed down sufficiently so that neither of these calamities occurred, although they had narrowly missed hitting a parked aeroplane. And they stepped out unharmed and very happy to be down. The whole story showing an incredible piece of airmanship and guts from the three of them.

They found that they had landed at Cranwell, from where their intelligence officer telephoned me after he had debriefed the crew and got the whole story. We sent a Wellington down next morning to collect them from Cranwell, and they were given a week's leave immediately. I also telephoned the AOC, first thing in the morning, to tell him the story personally and to ask for special and immediate awards for gallantry to be given to all three. The AOC agreed right away, and said he would recommend Sloan for the Conspicuous Gallantry Medal, the highest award any non-commissioned man could receive in the RAF other than, and ranking immediately after, the Victoria Cross. The navigator would be recommended for the DFC, and the wireless operator the DFM.

These all came through in a signal from Group HQ a few days later, and I was to read out the awards to the cheers of those assembled in the camp cinema where many were watching a film when the signal arrived. And of course we sent telegrams to the three recipients who were on leave. Sergeant Sloan was also given a Commission in the Field for his outstanding leadership and resolution, a great honour in itself. And finally he was also given an immediate place on the next possible pilot's course, which deservedly rounded off a really remarkable exploit.

Around this time, there was a lot of speculation and rumour that the enemy had captured a Wellington intact, or had at least rebuilt one, and were infiltrating it into the bomber stream and shooting down our unsuspecting aircraft as opportunity presented itself. The fact that this would have been almost impossible made no difference, the rumour persisted and gained much credence among the crews. It was difficult enough for a much faster night fighter with all the necessary radar aids and ground control assistance, both to get in among the bombers and then pick up an individual bomber to attack. But our losses were high enough for our crews to pick on something and make a myth of it to explain away some of them at least.

The truth was, of course, that some of our rear gunners were getting a bit twitchy, and before waiting to make positive identification would hose off at shadowy aircraft behind them and pump off streams of ammunition, believing that they were being trailed by enemy fighters. With our numbers increasing all the time, and concentration of the bomber streams getting tighter as well, some gunners were blasting off at shadows before they themselves were blasted. It is hard to condemn them, but they should have known the difference between a four-engined bomber and a twin-engined fighter even on a dark night, and it was more than tough on the recipients of this mis-applied zeal. Too often crews had to report being fired on by Lancasters or Halifaxes, and it was not at all funny to have this additional hazard added to all the others. A number of aircrew were wounded and aircraft damaged in this way, and God only knows how many were actually shot down – there must have been some.

The classic example of this was when sergeant pilot Aaron of a Stirling squadron was shot at by a fellow Lancaster, with the first burst coming straight in through the cockpit window wounding him seriously in the face and shoulders. He slid his aircraft away from the stream of gunfire and although gravely injured kept at the controls. They suffered another burst shortly afterwards, having had the great misfortune to have stayed behind the offending gunner in spite of having taken avoiding action. This second burst wounded Aaron again and he passed out. He was carried to the rest bunk and given a shot of morphine from the first aid kit to relieve his suffering, and somehow, with the aid of the automatic pilot one of the crew managed to get the aeroplane back to North Africa.

Aaron had recovered consciousness by this time, and insisted that he be carried back to the pilot's seat to make the landing, in spite of the fact that he had lost an eye and had been badly wounded in the chest as well. He made a safe landing and passed out again immediately, but his crew was saved. Aaron died very soon after, sad to say, but he was awarded the VC for his very gallant action in returning to his post and saving his crew and aircraft although mortally wounded.

From the debriefing reports of the night's operation, it

was discovered which crew had reported firing on a night fighter at the same time at which Aaron's navigator had logged their own attacks, and it was not difficult to pinpoint the culprit. He would have been court-martialled for gross negligence if that crew had not gone missing by the time the investigations had been completed. So here was yet another unpleasantness which our crews had to expect from now on, additional to the chances of collision already beginning to be increasingly experienced.

I have already described two occasions when wheels-up belly landings had to be made, and at Burn we had another one when a Wellington crew returning at dawn on a beautiful summer morning reported that they could not get their undercarriage down and would be making a wheels-up landing. I asked the pilot if there was any other damage and if the crew were all right, and he replied that everything was fine except for the undercart, with the flaps working properly. I told him that he would have to land last, and then to keep to the grass alongside the runway, to fly as slowly as possible to the last levelling out, and allow the aircraft to settle completely stalled, with both motors switched off at the last second and the control column hard back in his stomach. He was a very new pilot, and I felt it necessary to be so explicit in the most relaxed tone I could use.

It was now full daylight so we watched the whole performance from the control tower balcony. The young sergeant pilot made a finely judged approach, and set the Wellington down absolutely perfectly as told, throwing up sparks as it slithered across the hard surface of one of the runways, and coming to rest with no more damage than the normal bent-back airscrew blades and torn underside.

The aircraft was repaired and flying again in a few weeks. A somewhat happier incident than most, but definitely a 'good show' on the part of the young pilot. But sometimes these occasions could be a bit fraught because of badly damaged aircraft, failed engines, or wounded crew members

– and occasionally all three.

On 24 July, our Wellingtons of 431 Squadron were detailed to join in the full scale attack on Hamburg, and this time we were issued for the first time with boxes filled with packets of metallised strips of paper which had to be pushed down the flare chute at a certain point on the track out, from then on continuously until that point was reached again on the way home.

This was code-named 'Window', and we were told that as these packets scattered out in the slipstreams, they would create reflector clouds, distort enemy radar scanners and interfere with both the night fighter ground controllers and the airborne radar carried inside their fighters. Very happy to be trying out something really useful, the crews obliged with a will and proved the theory to be absolutely correct, the loss rate that night being very much lower than usual, and continued so for several nights thereafter. Post-war examination of the enemy's own reports for that night showed that the defences had been completely disrupted to the point of chaos, and taken completely by surprise.

This had been the launching of the series of massive attacks on Hamburg which was joined by the USAAF by day, when the city was bombed to ruins over the course of about ten nights and days, on the third or fourth night of which produced the dreadful 'Fireball', which awed even the most experienced of our crews when they witnessed it. The burning became so hot that hurricane force winds were created as air was sucked in from the surrounds to the scorching centre, and creating a volcano-like eruption, devastating everything in its path with the ferocity of the hot winds. This catastrophe was recreated to a somewhat lesser degree again and again on many other German cities as the war progressed. Having sown the wind, the enemy were literally to reap the whirlwind at the hands of Bomber Command until the bitter end.

Incidentally, we learned later that Window had been

available for use quite a long while before that night, but a War Cabinet decision had prevented us from doing so earlier as they were afraid of retaliatory use by the enemy to gum up our own radar defences. But since our bomber effort was so much greater than that of the Luftwaffe which was by now confined to very small and sporadic raids largely by fighter-bombers in hit and run attacks only, the advantage lay very much in our favour.

The enemy did in fact try out a type of Window after this, but it was somewhat different from ours and much less effective. They did not use it much. Their greatest effort went into finding counter-measures, and this they did quite successfully although we went on using Window right through to the end with reasonable results.

In fact the technical counter-warfare was being waged by both sides now, with increasing intensity. We were trying to protect our bombers by interfering as much as possible with their airborne radar and ground control systems. We even formed a separate group in Bomber Command. This was entirely devoted to carrying jamming equipment while they either mingled with the bomber stream, or 'stood off' over the seas round the enemy coasts listening, jamming and generally interfering with radar and signals traffic concerned with their night fighters, while the enemy were intent on getting round our jamming and other counter-measures. We had one splendid unit on the ground in this country which tuned in to the German ground controllers giving R/T instructions to their night fighter pilots while steering them into the bomber stream or telling them to go to some other area, giving them courses to fly and so on. Using very powerful radio transmitters on the same frequencies used by the enemy, our German-speaking operators were giving counter instructions to the wretched pilots, telling them to take no notice of the other instructions they had just received, and so on, with a slanging match developing between the two sets of operators. The chaos they created sometimes, with orders, counter orders, and argument going on between controllers, half of which was phoney, and the confused pilots not knowing which to believe, can easily be imagined. The poor pilots eventually not knowing their own backsides from their elbows could not possibly know what to do next except land at the nearest flare-path.

I had been over to Snaith on stand-down evening shortly after leaving for Burn, for a delayed farewell party, when that wretch Charlie Porter had taken my brand-new and proudly worn 'scrambled eggs' Service hat, (so called because of the gold oak leaves on the peak), and filled it with beer for everyone to drink out of. It never looked quite the same thereafter. But during July and August I had to go over there quite a lot as their Station Commander had been posted and a new one did not arrive for some weeks, so I had both stations to look after on days when operations were being prepared. And it was on one of those days when we were relaxing in the mess immediately after lunch and I was half asleep behind a newspaper, when there was a sudden tremendous double explosion at a split second interval, which came from the airfield in the direction of the bomb dump. I leapt out of my chair with heart pounding, and darted to the window, noticing two or three behinds disappearing under the billiards table as I did so, and we saw a large, ominous column of smoke rising from the bomb dump area into the clear summer sky.

Grabbing hold of the armament officer who was also in the mess, we piled into my car and raced down to the dump, picking up the ambulance and fire tender *en-route*. Five hundred yards from the entrance we met a white-faced airman running like the clappers away from it. Stopping him I learnt that he had been inside the dump at the time, but in a sand-bagged protection bay, and had therefore missed the blast. He said that he thought that at least two complete trolley loads of bombs had gone off, and I told the ambulance to take him off to the sick quarters for a medical check and treatment for shock.

The armament officer and myself then climbed the earth-works surrounding the dump and peered gingerly over the top to take stock. There was some heavy gauge ammunition which the blast had set off, and which was burning with much crackling and popping and creating a miniature but lethal firework display. And there was a huge crater in the middle of the tarmac area where the various bomb bays led off from the centre of the dump, with a very dead airman lying at the lip.

Standing nearby was another full trolley load of bombs which appeared to have been fused already, and this was where the danger lay, because it was quite probable that being so close to the explosion 'sympathetic detonation' might well have taken place and the bomb fuses been made live by the previous explosion. Most of the fuses were delayed action, while any of them could be set off by vibration if I ordered the fire tender and ambulance on to the site, so I was in a hell of a quandary. There would also have been other trolley loads of bombs out of our line of vision. We knew that sympathetic detonation had already occurred because one mis-handled fuse had already exploded two whole trolley loads of bombs as well as the Smith Gun ammunition, and I could not order the fire tender and ambulance crews into such an unstable situation. Those who had been near the explosion could not possibly have survived and I could not subject a further eight or ten men to the likelihood of a similar fate.

I decided therefore to leave things as they were until the bomb disposal experts had examined the situation, and immediately telephoned Group to that effect, asking for their bomb disposal team to be sent along 'soonest', and this was agreed. But a further complication was that a main railway line ran right along the outside edge of our bomb dump, and we feared that a train rattling by might again set off any of the disturbed fuses, so we had to drive round to our local halt – which itself was not far from the bomb dump – to warn the official in charge as to the situation. He was the ticket collector, porter, guard and station master all rolled into one, it being only a small country station, and we found him – quite understandably because of the popping and banging still emanating from the dump – on his hands and knees underneath the solid table in the ticket office.

We explained the facts to him and suggested that the Hull-Leeds line should be closed down until the matter had been cleared up, for if another load went off just as a train was passing, it might well cause a derailment. He put the suggestion to his office at York who naturally were a bit dubious, but I told them to telephone Group HQ themselves to get confirmation, and this was done.

It had been a most unnerving experience as far as I was concerned, and sixteen of our armourers had been killed because of the carelessness of one. Several of them had just disappeared altogether. Luckily this type of calamity did not happen very often, but several similar accidents did occur in bomb dumps over the course of hostilities, when over-confidence or carelessness resulted in tragedy.

In November, some re-shuffling in the Group was going on. The three-station group bases were being formed, with an Air Commodore in command at the main station of each base and two satellite stations forming the base of three. No 431 Squadron, which had quite a few Canadians in it already, was to be transferred to the new all-Canadian Group further north, and the English element of the squadron were to reform with one of the flights of 51 Squadron to make a Halifax squadron at Burn. I was detailed to go and take command at Driffield in East Yorkshire, which was the base station for Driffield, Leconfield, and Lissett, with an Air Commodore in overall command.

I didn't really want this, as I felt quite settled at Burn, and I knew that Driffield did not have a squadron at the time because concrete runways and dispersals were being put down there and the work had only just started, so it would be some months before it became operational. Neither did I relish having a superior HQ on the doorstep after my unfortunate experience at Abingdon.

In the event my fears were groundless: the Air Commodore and the Base HQ staff did not interfere with the running of the station in any way, and in fact all acted as if they were really station personnel rather than a different unit. All of which was highly satisfactory, with everyone working well together. And actually this posting probably did me a bit of good, because I had been in command of an operational squadron and/or station for eleven months, when the pressures and anxieties had been almost the same whether on the ground or in the air, with the constant mental burden of worry and responsibility when things went wrong. When added to my previous stint of fifteen months in 1940 and '41, this made another non-operational spell while runways were being constructed, probably of some therapeutic value for me, and may well have been why the AOC decided to move me.

Because we had a lot of spare accommodation at that time, Group had organised an Aircrew Commando Course at Driffield as a toughening-up and fitness scheme, and also to keep crews occupied while awaiting their conversion course to the Halifax II. So quite soon after my arrival there, two Free French squadrons were attached for the course. They were a good bunch of chaps, somewhat older than our own crews and with more flying experience, and it was rumoured that some of them had even flown against us from North Africa. They had apparently recently arrived from that area which had just been purged of the enemy. Many of them could not speak a word of English. We had great fun on the evening before they left us when we had a farewell party for their officers in the mess, which developed into a typical cheery thrash-up. Trying to translate some of our bawdy songs into French for their benefit was absolutely hilarious, and the Gallic versions in basic schoolboy French of 'Three old ladies locked in the lavatory' and 'Please don't burn our outhouse down' etc. were really quite something. Some of the rather bewildered French *aviateurs* even tried to join in and seemed to be enjoying the fun, although they must have thought that we were completely mad.

They did very well on their own station in 4 Group, frequently being top of the league in the air training results – bombing practice always continued whenever possible even on operational stations. I also heard later that in the vicinity of this French enclave, the local population of the common garden snail was very rapidly reduced to nil.

Another interesting diversion while I was here took place after I had a visit from the Brigade Major of the Brigade of Guards, Major Jock Hennessy, a Royal Tank Corps division being stationed in East Yorkshire for their pre-invasion training. They were asking for the use of some of our facilities for an exhibition of tanks, armoured fighting vehicles, and modern fighting transport and equipment generally. Group had warned me about it and asked us to give them full co-operation, and of course with our empty hangars we were able to oblige to their complete satisfaction. General Montgomery was to come and address the troops, and some of our airmen were allowed to attend also. They would not encroach on our hospitality by using our mess for lunch, but asked if we had a suitable hall where they could feed a hundred or more officers. Our crew briefing room was ideal, and they brought along their own field kitchen, cooks, and waiters so that they could do everything for themselves. The Air Commodore and I were invited to the lunch and were lucky enough to be seated right opposite to Monty. General Adair was there too, and was a most likeable personality. The whole event was extremely interesting and enjoyable, and I must say that the Guards certainly know how to do things in style.

I was being used as a general dogsbody all this time, as the AOC tried to keep me busy with odd jobs. One of these was to be sent off to various Yorkshire industrial towns to show the flag during their 'Wings for Victory' money-raising functions. Speaking to the public in town centres and exhorting them to cough up their 'brass' to buy bombers, was a new experience and both enjoyable and amusing. I also found that in spite of the rigours of war, the various mayors' parlours could still lay on an excellent lunch with plenty of spirits and wine thrown in, and these were always cheerful functions.

There was also a conference in London I was detailed for. Chaired by 'Cat's Eyes' Cunningham, a couple of our night fighter experts, a couple of bomber chaps, and a boffin or two made up the party to discuss night fighter tactics and operations. They seemed interested to have comment from the bomber viewpoint as they were not getting much practice over England in those days, and had to start going out among our bombers to try and sort out some of the Luftwaffe night fighters prowling among us. Which they did with a certain amount of success too.

A week's course at Porton Down Gas Warfare School was another job I was lurked for, and this again was quite interesting, until the grand finale that is, when we were all shut in a concrete hut with no windows, and subjected to a gas attack with chlorine gas for two minutes. We all emerged spluttering and retching to retire miserably to our rooms for a cup of tea and lie-down, which was most necessary. We still felt a bit the worse for wear at dinner that evening, but afterwards someone suggested that the best antidote might be the intake of a couple of scotches. With three cheerful American officers on the course, the two doses soon became more, and we only stopped when the whole whisky ration for the month had disappeared. But the medicine had worked all right.

By the end of March 1944, the runways at Driffield were nearing completion, and I was beginning to look forward to having a squadron allocated for operations to start once more, but just when all seemed ready another change-round occurred. Our Base Commander was posted, and John Whitley was to come in from commanding the station at Lissett to be our new Air Commodore. An Australian squadron had been earmarked for Driffield, so naturally they wanted to find an Aussie Group Captain to command the station. I was therefore sent over to Lissett to take over command there, and I duly arrived on 10 April.

John Whitley had first come into 4 Group as a Station Commander some two years previously, and because he had no operational experience he went fairly regularly on operations as second pilot to get that bomber experience which he rightly felt that he ought to have as Commander of an operational station. But he always took the precaution – which very few did – of carrying with him on those flights a small case holding a razor, toothbrush, socks, boots for walking, soap, and other odds and ends which would come in useful if he had to bale out over the other side at any time, as he was determined to try and avoid capture if this should happen. And one night it did. He was able to get out of the Halifax complete with ditty-bag, landing in the garden of a private house somewhere in Northern France. So he immediately buried his parachute and obvious flying kit, shaved off his RAF type moustache, and proceeded with his own personal evasion scheme. He could speak perfect French, having family connections in France and spent much time there pre-war, which was a tremendous advantage. And he did avoid capture, got in touch with the French Underground movement, and after an adventure which would almost make a book in itself, eventually reached Spain, freedom and repatriation, returning to 4 Group a few months later to carry on where he left off. A very fine type of officer.

The famous – or perhaps infamous – Nuremburg raid had taken place only twelve nights before I moved over to Lisset, when No 158 Squadron which was stationed there had lost four crews, and the Command itself over ninety on the worst night ever for the Command. Two separate books have already been written about this raid, and it is only necessary to mention here that the basic causes for the high loss rate on that night were first of all that bad weather with very high winds over the Continent – which had not been forecast or anticipated – seriously affected the bomber stream concentration, which rapidly became scattered and dispersed. Then there had been some disagreement among the Group and Command chiefs as to the route to be taken. Finally there was a lucky guess by the Commander of the German defence forces that night, who refused the bait of the spoof attack in a different area, and so managed to get the whole of his fighter force in amongst the bombers early for once, with near disastrous results to the Command.

CHAPTER SEVEN

Maximum Effort

ONCE again I found myself in the thick of things at Lissett. No 158 Squadron was in good shape under Wing Commander Jock Calder whom I had known previously. He was halfway through his second tour, and had become a Squadron Commander, before his twenty-third birthday. An exceptional young officer and fearless bomber pilot.

Operations had been ordered on the day I arrived, and unhappily four crews were lost that night. This was almost inexplicable as it was a French marshalling yard at Tergnier which had been the target, with only quite a short distance to go inside from the coast, and this type of target was normally thought to be somewhat less dangerous than those well inside Germany. But somehow a bunch of enemy night fighters got in amongst the bombers at the right moment for them, and quite heavy casualties were caused. A second attack on the same target a week later was more successful from the results aspect, but once again some fighters got at the bomber stream and created a certain amount of havoc, with 158 Squadron losing two more crews. An 18% squadron loss rate on that one target was an unfortunate start to my command at Lissett, but clear runs after those two raids for the next couple of operations, helped to restore the balance.

The squadron had recently been equipped with the newer Halifax III, the latest mark to come out of the factories, in which the Merlin engines had been replaced by four Bristol Hercules air-cooled radial engines of much greater power. These engines, coupled with the redesigned and more streamlined nose section, had improved the Halifax performance tremendously. I remember exclaiming in alarm on watching the take-off that first night at Lissett as each aeroplane climbed steeply away from the runway when it left the ground, instead of staggering off in almost level flight and climbing slowly up as the Mark II used to do. Sam Weller, one of the Flight Commanders, and Jock Calder who were in the control tower with me at the time, were both highly amused at my alarm, explaining that we now had a really good aeroplane.

I could hardly wait to get my hands on one to try it out, and after about three weeks when I had settled in I managed to 'borrow' one which needed a test flight. This was the first Halifax I had flown for just about a year, as the only aeroplane available to me at Burn and Driffield had been the little Tiger Moths which were the station communications aircraft, and only a delightful toy as compared to the bigger types. So this was a real treat and I enjoyed every minute of the forty-five it took for the test. I was most impressed with the Mark III. It handled well, had plenty of power in reserve, and no vices. It also looked good, and with its big, powerful engines and clean lines was a real beauty. The crews were very happy with them too, which was of great importance. So we now had an aeroplane every bit as good, if not better than, the Lancaster, which to our chagrin in 4 Group always seemed to get the glory from the media.

Not long after my arrival, our aircraft were landing back one night when a pilot called up control on R/T while he was taxiing back to dispersal, to report that there was an obstruction on the runway. By this time another aircraft had landed, and the pilot called up to say that there was a bomb on the runway, which he had struck with one of his wheels. I told the controller to keep all the remaining aircraft circling, then dashed out to investigate taking three of the crash tender crew with me in my car.

Sure enough, near the end of the runway was a dirty great 2,000 pounder lying half way across it, and I had to make a quick decision. I had no way of knowing if the damn thing was 'safe' or 'live', but if it was live it was possible that one of our aircraft would set it off if it was struck again, or even perhaps by the vibration if blown about by slipstream from the engines. So it just couldn't be left there in case an aircraft and crew were destroyed. All this went through my head in a split second, and I had no one to discuss matters with even if there was the time to do so. It just had to be removed, so I took a deep breath and told the three airmen with me to start rolling.

Together we rolled the blasted object off the runway and on to the grass, and since it didn't go off with a bang, we kept on rolling it across the perimeter track, then more grass to the side of the airfield, and plopped it into a small stream which ran along the boundary, a distance of perhaps 60 or 70 yards all told.

I had my fingers well and truly crossed all the time, hoping that it would behave itself, and fortunately it did. I thanked my helpers while taking them back to flying control, but they never knew of course that I hadn't had a clue as to whether it was as safe as I had had to pretend. But I had felt more than anxious for those few minutes. My gremlins had been looking after us again, and the armament officer exploded the bomb where it lay the next morning.

By now Bomber Command was completely involved in the more tactical role of softening up the areas which were going to lie directly ahead of the second front invasion which we knew must be started before long. Cracking at the coastal defence sites, the communications network of road and rail bridges, French marshalling yards and so on, in order to create as much disruption and chaos as possible in the rear of the German armies once the balloon went up. Of course we couldn't concentrate on any one area in order not to give anything away, so to keep them guessing we attacked a wide range of targets all along the Continental coast and inland, from Holland to Brittany.

Attacking these types of target was so much more practical and possible now than in earlier years, as the 'Oboe' equipment carried by the Pathfinder Marker aircraft and used in conjunction with a radio beam, made the marking of small targets both feasible and accurate. So from now on, interspersed with the normal strategic long distance bombing role, Bomber Command was called upon to carry out more and more of this tactical bombing, including close support for the invasion armies on the ground once the beachheads in Normandy had been established. And these were very welcome diversions for the crews at this time from the established 'rabbit runs' across Germany, since the losses were much lower except for a few rare occasions of which mention was made a short while ago. Our aircrew could at long last begin to feel, however tentatively, that there was a good chance of getting through a tour of operations now.

We had an American in the squadron at this time, Flying Officer Bob Cossor, who had joined up in the RAF before America officially entered the arena. But now that his country was an ally, they had been after him to leave the RAF and enter the USAAF, and this he had steadfastly refused to do until he finished his tour of ops with Bomber Command. However, the pressures on him got so great that he agreed to it eventually if the US authorities would compromise and allow him to complete his tour with 158 Squadron. And so it was arranged, since he was well on the way through his tour anyway.

So he disappeared on special leave one day, returning a few days later in the uniform of a US Air Force Lootenant. But the huge joke to his own crew and to all in the squadron, was that like everyone else on their first tour, he had no medals to show as an RAF officer when he went away, but on his re-appearance in USAAF uniform there was now a full row of ribbons under his flying brevet. No one could quite understand what they were all for, only that one of them was for just 'going overseas'. He took a lot of ribald comment with very good humour. A fine chap, well liked by all, and soon finished his full tour with us, being awarded the British DFC – the pride of his 'collection'.

Another example of an aircraft crashing on take-off occurred about now, engine failure forcing the pilot, Warrant Officer Collins, to switch off and retract his undercarriage before he got airborne. No one was hurt, and the aircraft did not catch fire, so all was well even though the fuselage was badly 'bent'. With the crew unscathed and no burn-up, this was almost considered to be a minor event in those days.

Jock Calder finished his second tour and was posted away, and Wing Commander Peter Dobson came in to command the squadron. I had known him before too, and was very pleased to get him as the Wing Commander. He had also completed a very successful tour in 4 Group previously, and was therefore fully experienced as well as being a highly efficient pilot technically.

Around this time crews were reporting strange small circles of light darting through and among the bomber streams at great speed, and sometimes with a slight 'tail' to the light. There was of course much conjecture as to this phenomenon, and we eventually decided, at our level, that it was some sort of controlled anti-aircraft rocket device. Having no knowledge of our own jet fighter development, which was highly secret of course, we had nothing to go on, although our guesswork turned out to be quite near to the truth when we were eventually told of the German experiments with rocket-propelled and jet-engined fighters. Luckily there were not very many of them.

For a considerable time now the Luftwaffe night fighter defence system had been operating at the peak of efficiency, and accounted for the great majority of bomber losses. God knows they got enough practice, and our crews reported many combat sightings nearly every time out, while our own 158 Squadron was receiving its fair share of interceptions too. But our gunners were fighting back, and the Command as a whole took a considerable toll of the enemy in the bitter air battles being fought out almost nightly. One of our difficulties was that enemy fighters were fitted with cannon which far out-ranged our puny .303 Browning guns in our own turrets, and so they could shoot at us while still out of range from return fire, and often without having been seen at all by our gunners. Also, the Luftwaffe had developed a system of mounting a cannon in their twin-engined fighters which could be aimed almost vertically upwards. This meant they could creep right up underneath a bomber and well below, shielded by the dark background, then suddenly pump cannon shells vertically upwards into the belly and wing stubs where the bombs and petrol tanks were situated in bombers, thus achieving complete surprise for their attacks. Nevertheless our gunners still had their own moments of success quite frequently too.

As has been mentioned, targets in Northern France could get as rough on occasions as those in Germany, so no relaxation of vigilance could be allowed. For example, one night raid on Trappes marshalling yards near Paris was a case in point, when a running air battle against fighters was fought out in bright moonlight. Although the enemy scored heavily that night, one of our own gunners – Sergeant Cripps – gave a long burst at a fighter whose aim was not too good and who got too close for his own health. It was then seen to go down in flames.

The star performers for the squadron that night, however, were Australian Pilot Officer Bancroft and his crew. Attacked by a Ju88 on the return journey, they received a very accurate burst of cannon fire right amid-ships in the belly which started fierce fires in the bomb bay and inside the fuselage, severely wounding the wireless operator. There was a large hole in the floor above the bomb bay and another in the nose area, while much damage had been done inside the aircraft as well. The hydraulic system had been shattered causing the flaps and bomb bay doors to fall down, while the gun turrets would no longer function. To make matters worse the starboard engine caught fire too, but happily this died down when they switched off the engine and feathered the 'prop'.

With petrol spewing out of the shattered feed pipes on the port side, the crew set about fighting the fires in the shambolic interior, and after using up all the extinguishers, had to finish the job by stamping and beating out the now reduced flames with booted feet and gloved hands, finally managing to subdue the fires completely.

In the process of avoiding further attack and recovering from the onslaught, the aircraft was now down to 2,000ft, and Bancroft was at last able to take stock of their situation which in RAF parlance was more than somewhat dodgy. With full flap on and bomb doors open – drastically reducing their speed – one engine useless, two great holes in the belly, the stink of burning electrics and other fittings still all-pervading, plus a howling cold draught of wind as well, they discovered to their consternation that three of the crew were missing. The wounded wireless operator had either fallen out or deliberately baled out of the front hole, and the flight engineer and mid-upper gunner were presumed to have fallen or jumped through the gaping hole amidships, possibly while fighting the fires.

Bancroft carefully nursed the cruelly damaged Halifax across the Channel, steering by the North Star because his compass was out of commission, and eventually calling for aid over the R/T which luckily was still working. He finally succeeded in crash-landing safely at Hurn near Bournemouth without injury to the remaining crew, although the Halifax was a complete write-off.

On top of this, the squadron lost five more crews that night, and out of a small force of only one hundred and twenty-eight bombers on Trappes no fewer than sixteen were lost altogether, all from 4 Group. There had been several other raids that night on targets roughly in the same area and with similar numbers employed on each, but they had received virtually no casualties at all, the whole weight of the enemy night fighter effort having been concentrated on the Trappes area, which was damned bad luck for the 4 Group squadrons.

Another Aussie rear gunner, Flight Sergeant Brookes, shot down a German twin-engined night fighter around this time during an attack on the Panzer barracks at Bourg Leopold in Belgium. He had spotted it stalking a friendly bomber, and opened fire at the same instant as the fighter. He saw flames streaking back from both friend and foe as they fell away downwards, so his intervention had been just too late to save our bomber, but at least he had taken revenge.

For the night of 5 June we briefed the crews that the Command was to put up over 1,000 aircraft on attacks against the Continental coastal batteries and strong points on a wide front between Ostend and Cherbourg, and we ourselves sent twenty-three from the squadron to join a force of one hundred-odd to bomb a defence emplacement on the Normandy stretch. There was nothing very unusual in this except that the numbers were perhaps a little higher than ever before, as the coastal strip had been visited in strength several times previously.

As the crews landed back, however, there was a buzz of excitement and speculation as they all reported having picked up on the radar screens of their H2S sets, a great number of blips from the English Channel, indicating that very many ships seemed to be on the way across. So we waited expectantly in the mess for the 7 o'clock news, confidently hoping to hear that D-Day had arrived and the invasion started. So imagine our consternation when there was no mention of anything of the sort, only the usual report that our bombers had been out in force again, in attacks on the German West Wall as it had come to be called. We all fervently hoped that this did not signify some sort of disaster, because we were absolutely certain that something momentous had been going on down there below during the night. And we just couldn't go to bed while waiting, anxiously now, for the next news at 8 o'clock, when to our joy we heard the historic BBC announcement that the invasion had begun with the landings in Normandy, that several beachheads had been forced and held, and that the battle was reported as going satisfactorily without the heavy losses which had been anticipated.

A tremendous cheer had gone up when we heard the news, although we had fully expected it, and everyone felt that this was at last the beginning of the end which could not be all that far off now. We could not perceive at that moment that a long, hard grind for almost another whole year lay ahead for the Allied Forces. On that night 1,043 bombers had been despatched on all those attacks, with only six crews missing from all these operations. Unfortunately the rather poor weather had interfered with accuracy, but our crews had done their best to help the armies of liberation on that historic occasion.

Just after D-Day the German 'Flying Bomb' campaign against London and the south-east of England started, with a ferocity which made it imperative for their launching sites to be attacked. The smaller and faster RAF and USAAF day bombers were put on to this job initially, because the sites were small, frequently hidden in woods and therefore hard to find, and in some instances mobile and continually moved around. And they became more than a bit of a nuisance, being a really nasty weapon, and it was decided that Bomber Command should have a crack at the 'Buzz Bomb' sites by day as well as at night.

There were some rather large permanent sites which needed attention, and with Allied superiority in the air by day now completely undisputed, it was considered reasonable to send the heavy bombers over in daylight with adequate cover from our own Fighter Command. So on 22 June 158 Squadron joined in the first daylight attack on a site at Siracourt in the Pas de Calais area. On the way down England they were to try and join up in as close a formation as they could as a protective measure if attacked by fighters. But since no practice formation flying had been carried out it was not very successful, and the aircraft on the outside edges of the formation had to release their bombs well off the target.

No enemy fighters were seen at all in fact, but a few accurate bursts of heavy flak were encountered at one point, when Peter Dobson's aircraft received a near miss which peppered the fuselage and deposited a piece of shrapnel in the calf of one leg. But in spite of the pain and discomfort he flew calmly back to base and made a perfect landing.

A more successful night attack was made on a major flying bomb site at Oisemont a few nights later, and then on 28 June the squadron was detailed for another daylight raid on an important site in a huge quarry at Wizernes in Belgium. I thought that I would like to take a look at this daylight lark myself to keep in flying practice, and the AOC had no objection. I took as my bomb aimer the squadron bombing leader, Flight Lieutenant Willie Turner. He had been with 78 Squadron when I had taken them over to Croft from Middleton St. George in 1941, and offered to come along with me for old times' sake. The rest of the crew were all sergeants.

It had been decided not to try and fly in formation any more, but in a loose gaggle so that aircraft could line up on the target individually as they did at night. The gaggle turned out to be so loose that even over the target there didn't seem to be anybody near us at all. It was a glorious clear summer day for a change, and all was quiet until approaching the target area a sudden burst of flak materialised dead ahead at about 150 yards distance. The only thing about it though was that this one was bright pink instead of the usual grey or black, and my suspicious mind decided that it was some sort of a signal to other gunners or to enemy fighters, as it was bang on our altitude.

So I veered off a little, and lost height slightly while we made a perfect run over the target which had been clearly marked by the Pathfinders and appeared to be receiving a pasting. It was a very successful attack by a small force of Halifaxes, and Willie got us a smack-on aiming point photograph.

Back at base again, Peter Dobson and Tom Parry, one of the Flight Commanders, were hugely amused at my taking evasive action for one burst of flak so far off the mark. But I told them that since it looked like a special signal, I was not going to get caught out at this late stage in the game, especially not on a picnic like this trip, and that the odd precaution could never come amiss.

Two days later the Command was asked to take a hand in the land battle round the beachheads of Normandy, when a medium sized force was given a target at Villers Bocage. This was an enemy strongpoint and key defence position in front of the British sector of the bridgehead, which was held by two crack Panzer Divisions preventing our troops from breaking out of Caen. Our squadron participated in this effort, when much havoc was caused to the enemy positions which was greatly appreciated by the army commanders and the troops too.

We had been bedevilled by unusually bad weather for much of June, and this continued on and off throughout July as well. Our crews were much hampered in their daylight efforts by this unseasonal meteorology, although in spite of it operations continued at high pressure with the Command trying to help the armies as much as possible. On many occasions now a night operation was ordered after a morning one on the same day, and both air and ground crews were kept exceptionally busy. And this was to be the pattern with occasional forty-eight hour 'rest' interludes in rotation until the final whistle blew. In other words the stations and squadrons in the Command were now operating at 'maximum effort' practically the whole time.

It must be said that the tremendous keenness and sense of duty of all the ground crews throughout the Command were vitally instrumental in our being able to keep up this pressure. There was seldom a day when one or more aircraft didn't need patching up ready for the next sortie a few hours hence, quite apart from the normal engine and airframe maintenance requirements between flights, and routine checks of every corner of each aeroplane. Much of this work was done at the dispersal points in the open and in all weathers, day and night. The ground crews would be at dispersals before the time of landing back from operations, waiting eagerly for 'their' aircraft to be taxied in, and they were desolate if it had gone missing and failed to arrive.

One fitter who needed a spare part for one of the engines, which was all that was needed to make 'his' aircraft serviceable, could not draw the item from the stores which had run out of that particular piece of equipment. So all the other necessary work having been completed by the evening, he quietly got on his bicycle and cycled 8 miles to Carnaby airstrip near Bridlington where he knew that one of our aeroplanes had landed in a badly damaged condition and was therefore completely unserviceable. He took the part he needed from the equivalent engine there, cycled the 8 miles back to Lissett, and worked through the night to finish the repair by early morning so that the aircraft could be reported serviceable for operations if required. A display of dedication typical of their motto which was: 'Difficulties quickly overcome, miracles take a little longer'. The Latin translation of this being – '*Ubendum – Wemendum*'. And they lived up to it.

Along with the ground crews must be included the WAAFs, who in their capacities as clerks, cooks, drivers, telephonists, instrument repairers, and even aircraft maintenance mechanics, did so much to help the squadrons and stations throughout the war, working long hours whenever necessary. There had been some mysogynists, of course, who predicted at the beginning when they started to come into the Service in large numbers, that they would have a disruptive influence and so forth. This was nonsense, and if anything theirs was a good impact on Service life. Naturally there were numerous 'affairs', but no more than at anywhere else in the country in those days. And there were many more serious-minded girls than the flightier ones, who nevertheless worked just as hard and well as any others. Many a lasting marriage was made by young couples who met while serving on the same unit during the war. The WAAF were a very great asset to the RAF, as were the women's branches of all the services, and as they still are of course.

We had rather an unlucky night when an attack on Caen

had been ordered. During take-off the sky was suddenly lit by a huge flash coming apparently from the sea a mile or so away behind the control tower, and moments later the next aircraft off reported on R/T that a Halifax was in the sea and on fire. There was nothing we could do then, but in the morning I went along to the coast with our engineer officer, Squadron Leader Tommy Rooke, to try and find out more about it.

The tide was out, but there was no sign of the aeroplane which must have been further out to sea. There was a coastguard standing at the top of the low cliff watching over five bodies which had been washed ashore during the night. The aircraft must have broken up on impact with the water to have released them. One had been cut right in half at the waist and the lower half was nowhere to be found, and they had all been washed clean by the sea – flying clothing included – but their faces were swollen and unrecognisable.

Their deaths would have been instantaneous however, and the whole incident so quick that probably only the pilot would have known for a split second that anything was wrong. We could only assume that the flaps had been selected 'Up' immediately after take-off, instead of the undercarriage, as this would cause the aeroplane to lose height rapidly and strike the surface of the sea, igniting the petrol as it broke up, even in the water.

All the other aircraft took off safely, but flak over the target was reported as being extra heavy that night, and two of our aircraft failed to return. A third landed back with over eighty holes of various sizes but miraculously with no harm to the crew, while we watched a fourth from the roof of the control tower as it carried out a hairy landing at Carnaby about 6 miles away as the crow flies, but which happily ended safely for the crew. Carnaby was one of those FIDO airstrips consisting of three extra long runways laid side by side, and built to receive large numbers of bombers on foggy nights when airfields were closed by bad visibility. But they were more often used to take in badly damaged aircraft which needed extra long runways for the pilots to be able to make safe landings.

As we had poor visibility at Lissett – although good enough to land undamaged aircraft – our fourth casualty that night had reported that they had received severe damage with one engine out of action too. So we sent him to Carnaby who were only too pleased to oblige, and lit up the fog dispersal flare path to help him. We saw his navigation lights circling at Carnaby and he went straight in to land, although approaching rather low in the final moments. In the light of the fires there we could see an engine suddenly burst into flames just before he sank out of our sight on to the runway, and waited impatiently for the telephone call from Carnaby we knew would be coming in a moment. It came soon to reassure us that the pilot had landed safely and the crew were all right, but that they had been so low in the approach funnel that the aircraft had struck the chimney of a disused farmhouse during the final approach, an airscrew had been knocked off, and the engine had caught fire. They had just scraped in over the boundary. Flying Officer Lennard had made a safe arrival in difficult circumstances on this, the last trip of his tour, and he and his crew were posted off to non-operational duties a few days later, after this exciting finish to their operational stint.

Another attack on the Villers Bocage defence system was laid on for the morning of 30 July, and I took a crew so that I could have a look at the beachhead and the Mulberry harbour at Arromanches for myself. Unfortunately the weather forecast was poor both at base and over the target but as the armies desperately wanted to break out the Command had to make the effort, and quite a large force was to be deployed. However the weather was even worse than expected, and after an early morning take-off we climbed straight into 10/10ths cloud at 1,000ft, emerging into bright sunlight shortly afterwards at 8,000ft. Continuing down England without a single break in the clouds below, we could see the cumulo nimbus piling up over the Channel to at least 15,000ft ahead of us.

As we approached ETA target, the Pathfinder Master-Bomber's urgent call of 'Down – Down – Down' came clearly over the headphones, so we pushed the nose down and opened the bomb doors hoping that the cloud would break sufficiently for us to get a look at the target, or at least give us a reasonable ceiling below which we could drop our load. But while we were still in cloud and still diving, the code word came through for the attack to be abandoned. It was most frustrating and a trifle alarming too, knowing that there were some 600 aeroplanes all doing the same thing in this thick cloud all around us. So I kept straight on for a while, then started climbing slowly and turned gingerly back on to a course for home.

There was still 10/10ths cloud at 6,000ft running up England, and calling up base on arrival there we heard that the ceiling was still only 1,000ft but with good visibility underneath. So we turned due east to break cloud over the sea, and then back to the airfield. Most disappointing. But the army certainly showed their appreciation for our efforts in hopeless circumstances, by sending a signal to our C-in-C thanking all the crews for trying. It must have been very frustrating for the army boys too, hearing all those lovely bombers going overhead but unable to see the ground to help them out by bashing a nasty strongpoint.

This happened on several occasions during that awful summer, and it seemed to us that the Almighty was on the side of the enemy. Given reasonably average weather over that period, I am sure that the Allied armies would have broken out of the bridgehead much sooner than they did. It is interesting to note that when we had made a successful attack in clear weather on an enemy strong-point in front of our troops, they had found in their own attack and advance immediately afterwards that the German troops were still huddled in shelters, absolutely dazed, deafened, and made irresolute by the magnitude and concentration of the bombing. In this way several strongly defended enemy positions were captured comparatively easily after Bomber Command had been able to give them a good thumping in clear weather first.

On the night of 7 August, our crews again took a hand in helping the ground forces in what was to be the great break-out from the beach-heads. All through the night heavy blows were struck at the crack Panzer groupings in front of our troops all along the line, and with great effect. The tremendous surge forward at Falaise began, starting the war of movement which took the Allies right through to Paris and Brussels. And for several days after the break out, small forces of bombers ranged ahead of our advancing troops in daylight, attacking enemy fuel, ammunition, and equipment dumps.

Reverting to our strategic role after this spate of tactical sorties, 158 joined in a heavy attack on Brunswick which brought the usual violent reaction from the enemy. We lost one crew that night on what was the last trip of their tour, a most tragic occurrence which unhappily took place on occasions. It was no uncommon event for a crew to get within two or three sorties to complete their quota only to go missing at that late stage. Four more of our aircraft were badly damaged that night, and one gunner was wounded slightly. One Halifax, piloted by Flying Officer Cowden, had a lucky escape from an attack by a fighter which had got in a quick burst at them. Flight Sergeant James Campbell, the bomb aimer, was soaked by hot coffee when his flask was hit and broke just beside him, while the rear gunner realised on landing that he had been luckier still. When examining his turret which had also been hit by the cannon shells, he found that one of the barrels of his guns had been bent to an angle of 90° while the whole turret was badly scored and pitted with shrapnel.

The armies were now moving forward rapidly on a broad front, with Normandy far behind and Cherbourg still having to keep the supply lines going, although the distances were lengthening and therefore now causing problems. Le Havre had been by-passed by the advancing Allies, but it was now imperative that this port should be captured in order to shorten the over-extended distances which the armies' supporting transports were now having to travel. And Le Havre was being tenaciously held by a very determined garrison and commander. So Bomber Command was called in to help, and from 5 September to 11 September carried out continual attacks on enemy defence positions in the countryside around Le Havre, and on 10 September I took Willie Turner again as bomb aimer with a complete crew of new junior officers to join in this shuttle service. In absolutely clear weather we had a good run over our particular target, almost as if on the practice ranges. The garrison commander had had enough after the next day's bombing, and surrendered to the 49th and 51st British Divisions on the 12th.

Many of the Bomber Command crews who had baled out over Northern France or Holland in the run-up to the invasion, and who had been succoured and hidden by the gallant Dutch, Belgian, and French Escape Organisations, were now being recovered by our armies and returned to England. As the Allies steadily advanced, surprising numbers were being freed as the ground troops over-ran their hiding places.

With so much daylight activity going on, I was sent down to Andrews Field, just north of London. This was a large Fighter Command station from where some of the fighters which carried out the protective cover on our daylight sorties, were stationed, and it was thought that some personal liaison might be a good idea. Andrews Field had been built by the Americans – hence the name – and had been handed over to the RAF when the USAAF squadrons moved to France. There was a Polish and a British wing there, both flying the famous Mustang long-range fighter.

Arriving early enough to attend briefing, we watched the take-off after a quick lunch, then back to the mess to wait for the landing and debriefing. They had not encountered any enemy fighters that day, so there was little to report. We had an early take-off to return to Lissett next morning, and after dinner in the company of an old friend I had met there, Wing Commander Bill Fleming, we repaired to the ante-room for a quiet sup of ale. The Polish squadrons were doing some night circuits and bumps, as training practice for the odd occasion when a night landing or take-off was operationally necessary. Some of those who were not flying started a bit of a thrash-up after the evening meal, and a lot of milling about and rough games went on for about an hour and a half, when it subsided as quickly as it had begun. Quite unlike our bomber boys, I thought in a rather superior way, because when we started a ding-dong it usually went on fairly late.

An amusing little bit of by-play had been enacted while all this was going on. A very handsome Polish Wing Commander, the wing leader of the Polish element and a Count by title, was standing at the bar quite close to where Bill and I were sitting quietly watching all the fun. The gallant Count was binding on a bit about the need for all this messing about in the air in the dark, and to add weight to his objections finished with the unarguably acceptable statement that 'Ze night vas made for Loff, and not for flying around in ze bloody aeroplanes' – a sentiment which was obviously heartily endorsed by a particularly good-looking Waaf officer who had been at his elbow all the time, and hanging on to his every word.

With the Allied advances going well, a special conference was called at Group attended only by Station Commanders and their senior navigation officers. In the strictest secrecy we were told of a proposed huge daylight raid being considered to finish off Berlin. The Americans were to take part as well of course, and with the right sort of planning it was thought that losses would be within acceptable limits. Over 3,000 aircraft would take part as a demonstration of Allied air power, and the magnitude of this daring conception caused quite a stir among those present.

Driving back to Lissett afterwards with Frank Stanyard,

my Squadron Leader navigator, I said that if it came it would be such an historic occasion that it would be a pity to miss it. He agreed, and said he would come with me if it did get laid on and I got permission to go. We said nothing to anybody when we got back, not even to Wingco Dobbie, but no more was heard of the scheme so it must have been shelved.

Early in October we were briefed for an attack on Cologne one bright moonlit night, and Dobbie slipped my name on to the crew list for me to participate, but the Base Commander, backed by the AOC, ordered me off it, and another pilot had to take the crew. I was a little disappointed but clearly understood the sense of it. The Command as a whole lost quite a number of Station Commanders on bomber operations, and while this was considered acceptable when those Group Captains had no previous operational experience, and very commendably wished to obtain such experience at first hand in order to be on terms with those they had to command, it was quite another matter when a Station Commander already had a tour or more of bomber ops behind him, and had 'got some in' as the saying went in those days.

With the tremendous expansion of the RAF generally, and Bomber Command in particular, it was getting more and more difficult to find officers senior enough in terms of years served to put in charge of stations, so those who qualified in that way and had got sufficient operational experience as well, were kept off ops. Those who were senior enough for command, yet who had not got bomber experience were encouraged to fly however – even as second pilot – until they had enough trips in for the crews to be able to regard them as one of themselves 'operational'.

But there was one over-keen type in another Group who insisted on piloting a Lancaster himself on being posted to command a station, and he was not qualified for four-engined aircraft. After only one rather hairy practice flight, he took a reluctant crew on an operation and killed them all – including himself and over this country too, through sheer inexperience of flying heavy aircraft. Brave perhaps, but foolish and selfish, as he could just as easily have gone as second pilot until he had received the proper instruction at a conversion unit.

On the other hand, we had a Station Commander in 4 Group, Group Captain Brookes, who had no bomber experience when he was posted as CO, who made it his duty to try and complete a tour of operations as second pilot, and flew regularly until he had achieved this. A very fine example of the right sort of leadership.

Another classic example of this sort of dedication was that of the RAF doctor who decided to specialise in 'Operational Fatigue among Operational Aircrew', and insisted that he could do this better by flying with the crews he was studying. He had been a very young pilot at the end of World War I and wore a pilot's brevet, but became a doctor between the wars. He therefore qualified and flew as an air gunner in order to participate fully on operations. Squadron Leader 'Doc' McGeown was a well-loved and admired member of the Command, who flew frequently with the Pathfinder squadrons.

With the daylight attacks now being conducted over heavily defended German targets, our crews were able to see what it must look like if they could see things at night time, and most of them wished that they hadn't had the opportunity! Although used to seeing the flashes exploding thickly in the barrages when approaching a target, once in it at night it didn't look so bad. But in daylight, the mass of smoke bursts lingering above the target with more being added all the time, was pretty awe-inspiring, and our admiration for our American counterparts increased accordingly. They had to plough through this visual mayhem in full daylight every time out.

Another ugly sight now being seen in full and awesome detail occasionally, was of bombers receiving a direct hit by flak and disintegrating in close proximity to others. At night all one saw was a sudden burst of flame which then curved slowly downwards to disappear in cloud or strike the ground far below. Somehow it was all rather impersonal. But now an exploding aircraft could be identified by those nearby and it all became so much more dramatic. A personal account might best illustrate this.

Sergeant J. Lewis, a flight engineer on the squadron at Lissett, reported that during a daylight attack on the Ruhr while he had no specific duty for a few moments, he stood looking through the astro-dome which was close to his post in the aircraft, surveying the scene around him. He was watching another Halifax about 200 yards astern, when it received a direct hit from a flak shell in the bomb-bay, and to quote his own dramatic description of what then happened:

'It bucked with the force of the explosion, and folded amidships right underneath the H2S blister but kept coming forward on an even keel. The two outer engines then literally pulled themselves out of the main plane and fell away forward in a gradual sinking movement. The crew then started to bale out, the rear gunner from his turret, two from the upper escape hatch, then two more from under the nose. Gradually the Halifax lost height and started to disintegrate, with the outer wing sections going first. The port inner engine then burst into flames trailing black smoke and balls of fire. Everything seemed to happen in slow motion, and the whole spectacle had a peculiarly macabre fascination. The debris surrounding the Halifax looked just like a wall diagram of a sectionalised bomber as it fell slowly from view holding its flight path. And the whole episode was virtually over in seconds.'

One night at this time we were woken up in the small hours by some unusual sounding aircraft noise, and in the distance inland an ominous crump or two. I telephoned the operations room to ask the duty officer what was happening to find out whether I should get up. But he explained that there was an air raid alert on, which had been sounded because a number of flying bombs had come in from out to sea. There was no apparent danger to us it seemed, as they had all gone inland, so I told him to telephone me if any further attacks appeared to be coming near us, and went back to bed.

We heard from Group next morning that a few flying bombs had been delivered into Yorkshire from enemy bombers out at sea, but they had all landed rather haphazardly at widely dispersed points in open countryside and little damage had ensued. One had landed close to our Group's airfield at Pocklington, and had by chance done some slight damage to a Halifax, but this seemed to be the sum total of a rather useless and extravagant effort from the Luftwaffe. The very next day the Army deployed a number of ack-ack units in a narrow strip along the Yorkshire coast in case this was to be a regular feature of enemy tactics, but it was never repeated.

The Command continued its attacks by day and night at full strength and momentum, and the huge German air bases at Gilze Rijen and Eindhoven in Holland were raided in daylight, being sandwiched between night raids into Germany. Daylight attacks on the Ruhr had been started, and 158 Squadron took part in the first one with twenty-one crews. On this highly defended area, which had normally produced fairly heavy casualties at night, it was feared that they might be even heavier by day, but happily this was not so and the enemy reaction was lighter than anticipated. Only one of our squadron's aircraft was damaged by flak, but the pilot, Flight Sergeant Powe, RAAF, successfully crash-landed his badly damaged Halifax at the Fido airstrip in Essex with only two engines functioning. A very good effort on his part.

With our armies now approaching Holland and the Rhine, it enabled the routing of bombers to be diverted away from the old rabbit runs across north-west Germany. This gave our crews much more time over friendly territory and away from the German fighter control zones and heavily defended flak and searchlight belts. All of which was a highly satisfactory state of affairs for our crews.

With the tempo of bomber operations at such a peak, however, with over 1,000 aircraft out nearly every time, and from 700 to 900 being the norm when really heavy attacks were required, there were still many casualties to come. The ratio of mid-air collisions which had slowly increased since 1942, was now becoming larger also, constituting a danger which was feared almost as much as the more normal hazards, by crews now privately calculating their more reasonable chances of surviving a tour.

One example should be sufficient to illustrate the dangers of the crowded air-space which faced large numbers of bombers flying in close company at night, although many more – seen and unseen – occurred throughout those years in 1943/44/45. It concerned a 158 Squadron Halifax during an attack on Hanover in January 1945, when Flying Officer McLennan's aircraft was rammed underneath on the run-in to the target. Sergeant Hibbert, the mid-upper gunner, thought that a Lancaster had hit them while taking evasive action when attacked by a night fighter, as he then saw a Lancaster go down out of control and on fire. The bomb aimer, Pilot Officer Carroll, was thrown to the floor by the tremendous jolt and pinned against the bombsight in the resultant dive. With an ice-cold draught blowing in he thought that the nose of the aircraft had been ripped off and that 'this was it'. His intercom plug had become disconnected, but he saw the navigator, Flight Sergeant Huband, struggling with the forward escape hatch, and then realised that he might be getting one more chance. And they were just about to bale out when the pilot called for everyone to stay put as he was pulling the aircraft out of the dive, and with this action the fearful vibration lessened.

One of the starboard engines then fell away, but McLennan held course until the bombs were dropped, and, still keeping to the main bomber stream for safety, turned with difficulty for home. All the instruments were useless, and there was a large hole in the floor of the nose section, while the nose itself was bent to starboard causing the aeroplane to tend to fly in circles. So in a freezing gale they struggled on, the navigator using his sextant to keep the pilot flying west on astro shots. As the English coast was approaching after a long drag home, they saw searchlights pointing towards the emergency landing strip at Woodbridge in Suffolk.

They now found that they could not lower the wheels, and furthermore to their horror realised that the 4,000lb 'cookie' was still in the bomb bay with its wire safety hawser still in place. They tried to chop through the wire by using the escape axe, but this was no use, and in desperation Huband pulled at an electric junction box and the great bomb fell away taking the bomb-bay doors with it. McLennan successfully crash-landed the aircraft shortly afterwards under those difficult conditions, when another engine fell off with a clatter as they were skidding along the runway and slithered to a halt on to rough snow-covered ground off the side of the flare-path.

As they all scrambled thankfully out, Sergeant Statham, the flight engineer, heard a frantic call for help from the rear end and running round found the young gunner, who was on his first trip, half suspended out of his turret having been firmly caught up in the mechanism by his flying boots, and quite unable to free himself.

They were all able to return to Lissett the next day except for the wireless operator, Sergeant Spivey, who, in spite of the intense cold immediately after the collision, had without hesitation stripped off his gloves and courageously worked at trying to repair the damaged wireless equipment, until his fingers became too swollen from frost-bite for him to be able to do any more. He received an immediate award of the DFM for this very brave action, and McLennan a DFC. All the crew had behaved magnificently during this hazardous episode.

Before take-off one night for a raid on Duisburg, Flight Lieutenant MacAdam had some difficulty with his starboard outer engine which showed a heavy 'mag-drop' during the running-up test. He taxied over to where a spare aircraft was standing ready and bombed up, to take that instead, but found another crew had beaten him to it. So getting back into his own aeroplane Mac felt that the doubtful magneto had now cleared sufficiently for him to be able to use the aircraft, so taxied to the take-off point.

They started off all right, but as the great bomber was about set for lift-off the starboard outer motor cut dead. In a split second he then did the only possible thing – selected undercarriage lever to the 'Up' position, and switched off all the engines. The Halifax remained airborne a few feet above the runway for an agonising couple of seconds, before it crashed down and screeched to a shuddering halt, catching fire immediately.

Only the rear gunner failed to get out quickly, and as he was missing when MacAdam checked his crew, the pilot went straight back into the fuselage to try and free him from the inside. Unable to do this, he nipped smartly out again and chopped the turret open to free the gunner, and all got away safely.

This all happened in moments, and I arrived out there just as the crew were walking away from the now crackling ammunition, and it wasn't long before the petrol tanks exploded.

MacAdam swears that I then said to him, 'The next time you bloody wild Scotsmen want to declare war on England, please don't pick on my damned airfield!'

I can't remember this at all because he had shown great determination in attempting to get into the battle, had instantly taken the correct action when things went wrong, and had behaved most courageously in freeing the trapped gunner. The crew were safe, that is what mattered, and in those circumstances aircraft were always expendable. If I did say it I have long since apologised, but it would only have been due to a thankful reaction that all the crew were safe.

By this time, after three years of close association with bomber operations, and having been heavily involved with a variety of dicey incidents and assorted prangs throughout these periods, I had developed a bit of a 'twitch' about watching the daily or nightly operational take-offs. The ritual of going down to the flying control tower or flare-path caravan to wave the chaps off had become something of a mental agony, and I had to make a very strong effort of will to get down to the airfield instead of waiting around in the ops room or in my office, pretending to be getting on with some paperwork. The burden of responsibility was almost as much of a strain now as actually flying had been.

Strangely though, watching the return from operations in the control tower was not nearly so traumatic, although many shaky do's occurred during this phase. With very little fuel, normally no bombs aboard, and the aircraft much lighter to handle, perhaps I felt that things were less lethal somehow, although this was not really borne out by past experience.

As if we did not have enough on our plate, we were suddenly called upon one misty mid-November afternoon, to prepare to accept a wing of the Eighth USAAF whose bases in East Anglia had been closed by thick fog. Luckily we had no ops planned for that night because the fog was expected to spread north. So they arrived, and in good order landed one after the other in quick time and without any assistance from our flying control. Their circuit and landing drill and discipline was immaculate. Twenty-four Flying Fortresses and Liberators of Lieutenant-Colonel John Grable's 448th Bomb Group (H) put down at Lissett, so we had over 200 extra aircrew to look after, feed and accommodate.

In common with all bomber stations we always had a spare barrack hut ready with beds and blankets for small diversions, but this was something else. Group had already agreed to send us extra drivers and transport to help us out, but when we realised from the Met reports that the fog would persist for three or four days, we had to ask for more cooks and aircraft-hands as well. We had enough spare beds and blankets in the stores, and luckily more barrack huts too, to prepare sufficient sleeping accommodation which we had been able to get ready before they arrived. And thereafter, for the next three days, our cook-houses were going full blast most of the time, the camp cinema was opened for morning and afternoon sessions as well as for the evening ones. Special aircrew buses ran an almost non-stop shuttle service to and from Bridlington for their extra entertainment. The Naafi manager opened up our comfortable Naafi Club all day for their use, and the officers' and sergeants' messes were open to them at all times of course. We even cashed cheques for their officers from the CO's Benevolent Fund, and there were no 'bouncers'. Luckily we could do no flying ourselves for those three days because the fog persisted all over England, so that was a blessing.

The whole of my station personnel rose magnificently to the occasion, falling over themselves to make things as comfortable as possible for our visitors. I was immensely proud of them all and grateful for their unstinting efforts, and told them so in a Tannoy broadcast when it was all over. Our guests were most appreciative too, and I still have the official letters of thanks and congratulation signed personally by Lieutenant-Colonel Grable and Colonel Charles B. Westover, their Base Commander at the time, from Major-General W.E. Kepner, commanding their 2nd Bombardment Division, and from Lieutenant-General J.H. Doolittle, the Commanding General of the US Eighth Air Force.

Throughout that winter of 1944/45, the operational pattern continued day and night, and although the loss rate had slowed down, we still had many aircraft coming back with varying degrees of damage. And yet another crew had a fatal crash not far from the airfield having just taken off on a training flight. We never found out the reason because the whole crew perished. Accidents from unknown causes were somehow harder to accept than those we knew more about, as we were always left wondering.

With the Allies along the Rhine, and then across it, and the Continent fully liberated, things were far from 'all over bar the shouting'. The mental agony of crews who could now reasonably expect to be alive at the end, must have been really awful each time they were ordered over some particularly well known hot spot. But they pressed on in their usual determined way, with no LMF cases, and no operations unnecessarily aborted. They were terrific, and I admired them more than ever. The standards and morale never fell right to the very end.

The reaction of Flight Lieutenant Jack Watson and his crew was typical of this, when a flak shell went straight through his aeroplane without exploding. However it had struck the bank of oxygen bottles *en-route*, and these did blow up, forcing a large hole in the side of the fuselage. At a temperature of -29° C the pilot continued with his bombing run, with the bomb aimer getting frost-bitten fingers in the process. The navigator, Flying Officer R.E. Kennedy, RNZAF, had all his maps sucked out through the gaping hole in the side, but together they made their way back to Carnaby and Jack Watson made a perfect and successful landing there. I was able to recommend, and give him, a Green Endorsement in his flying log book, an honour accorded to pilots for very special displays of airmanship in the handling of aircraft in exceptionally difficult or hazardous situations.

Another Green Endorsement was earned by Flying Officer Lapidge, RAAF, for superior airmanship displayed during a potentially dangerous situation when an engine packed up suddenly and inexplicably on the way to a target in Germany. He carried on to the target which was still some distance away, dropped his bombs, and carried on in the bomber stream for safety under reduced power and with some of his hydraulics out of action. He eventually landed back safely at base. A very fine effort.

I keep mentioning Dominion aircrews. From June 1941 in No 76 Squadron and onwards, I had many Australian, Canadian and New Zealand aircrew under my command. There were great numbers in Bomber Command particularly, as well as in all the other operational flying commands, and we could not have fought at such strength without them.

They joined in with their British counterparts in mixed crews, as complete crews in mixed squadrons, and in wholly Dominion squadrons and stations. The Canadians even had one Bomber Group to themselves. We always got on well together in my experience, and I am glad to have met and served with so many. They were great chaps. On many a pay day, the 'Canucks' would start a crap session on the billiards table in the sergeants' mess, and either lose all their pay in one evening, or win enough to put in for a 48 hour pass to go and spend it all on a binge in London!

Early in March 1945 our returning bombers were infiltrated one full moon night by a number of Ju88 night fighter intruders. All over the eastern part of the country from East Anglia to North Yorkshire the air raid warning 'red' was being given to our bomber stations. We received ours after we had landed only three or four aircraft, and we switched off our airfield lighting, ordering the other aircraft to divert to safer airfields inland, to turn off their own navigation lights, and to look out for intruders. At this moment we saw from the control tower the tell tale horizontal flashes of tracer cannon shells aimed at one of our bombers in the circuit only a couple of miles to the west, and at about 3,000ft. We were dismayed to see it catch fire and plummet to the ground. Our 'Red Alert' had come too late to save him, and there were no survivors.

A moment later the intruder made a pass along the runway where a Halifax had just turned off to go to dispersal, then it turned to port and came straight across the hangar behind the control tower. I had hurried outside after telling the duty controller to broadcast for all ground defence personnel to report to flying control at the double, and ordering all personnel on the technical site to go to shelters. I was therefore standing on the tarmac watching the impudent blighter pull out of his dive, and as he climbed away a stick of small but very nasty anti-personnel fragmentation bombs exploded just off the perimeter in an open field. At that moment too there was a clatter from the roof of the hangar a few yards in front of me, which indicated that something had fallen through it. The hangar doors were wide open, and as I hurried over, I saw clearly in the moonlight the ominous shape of a tall, slim bomb standing on its nose between two ready loaded bomb trolleys. They were standing ready there for loading on to an aircraft for an early morning daylight raid which we had to prepare for as soon as our aircraft had landed.

An inquisitive young airman had followed me into the hangar, but the moment he saw this rather ugly sight he turned and ran, shouting at the top of his voice in absolute panic, 'It's a bomb it's a bomb – there's a bomb in the hangar.' I raced after him, and being comparatively young still, and quite fit, caught up with him in seconds. I seized him by the collar, shook him until his teeth rattled and shouted at him to shut up. As he recovered, I told him to nip over to the duty control officer in the tower and ask him to Tannoy for the armament officer to report to me at No 1 hangar immediately, then waited at a reasonably safe distance but ready to duck smartly at the first crack of the delayed fuse which I expected would knock hell out of my hangar any moment now.

Flight Lieutenant George Harrison arrived very quickly, and together we approached the damned object, on tip-toe for the last few yards so as not to disturb it into action. As we crept gingerly round to the other side of the bomb, we simultaneously burst out laughing with relief. The dreaded 'bomb' was only half of a cylindrical container which had carried the smaller bombs already fallen. The mother case simply fell away from the intruder when the pilot pressed the tit, then automatically opened when a pre-determined time or distance had elapsed, allowing a cluster of extremely lethal anti-personnel bombs to shower out when near the ground. But the container itself was bomb-shaped, and we had been creeping nervously round it because only the one convex side was showing from the hangar doors.

But the situation was far from funny. The intruder was still around, and even as we ran back to the control tower it made a pass at it, pooping off its cannon in a most unfriendly way. Sheltering behind the building we saw little wisps of smoke spout up a few feet away where two shells thudded into the earth just in front of us. Then nipping smartly up the stairs to the control office I called up the last Halifax to land which still had its engines running, and told the pilot to keep one engine going so that the rear gunner could have a crack at the Ju88 if it came round again. Then back to the Tannoy to ask for any armament personnel who knew anything about our Bofors gun sitting idly among its sand-bags just asking to be used. There was no sign of any of our defence personnel, I should add.

I was in our tiny telephone exchange now just behind the flying control room, and asked the Waaf sergeant telephone operator to get me the local AA unit so recently deployed near us after the Flying Bomb incident. All this was taking place at high speed I should add, but meanwhile the wretched intruder was enjoying himself by making another pass at the flying control tower, breaking a window and putting a hole in the crash tender which caused the fire fighting chemical to leak away in a spurt of foam. But the Waaf telephonist was calmly sitting at her small console, attending to my instructions, although the window faced the direction of the attacks and she was therefore in some danger. She seemed to be a lot calmer than I myself felt, because I was beginning to get very angry that we were not able to hit back. My call to the army unit came through and I spoke to their duty officer.

Telling him that as the aeroplane he could undoubtedly hear and see flying round our airfield circuit at about 500ft, and occasionally shooting us up was an enemy Ju88 no less, in case his gunners couldn't recognise one, would he kindly arrange to have the bloody thing shot down. He replied that they were 'Only there for protection against flying bombs'. I got rather angry at that and shouted down the phone, 'Don't talk cock, an enemy aircraft is an enemy whether it has a pilot or not so ruddy well get on with it'.

His answer that he had not got the authority made things even worse. I repeated who I was, told him that I was senior to his own commander, that there were no friendly bombers in the vicinity, that I gave him authority and took full responsibility for the order, so get a bloody move on and shoot the bugger down. He said he would see what he could do, and I rang off absolutely fuming with rage and frustration.

Going outside again to see what was happening, I eyed the single Bren gun sitting forlornly on top of the Control Tower, but there was no ammunition with it. The intruder was coming down for another dive at the tower, but this time a stream of tracer was hosed up behind him from the Halifax I had alerted at its dispersal point across the airfield, and the armament warrant officer with a sergeant armourer were at the Bofors loading a clip of shells into the breach. After this last dive the Ju88 made a quick turn and came round on a reciprocal course over the technical site at about 200ft and flying straight and level as if he was examining the damage he hoped he had done – which was virtually nil as he was a rotten shot – and as it passed, over, the Bofors got in a quick and accurate burst. Standing right beside the sand-bagged emplacement I saw the flash as one of the tracer shells struck the blighter smack in the middle of the fuselage under the cockpit canopy just about where the navigator would be sitting. It rocked slightly and turned climbing away to port and out to sea, and we saw no more of it. At least he didn't get away scot free I thought bitterly. I could have hit him with a pea-shooter at one moment as he pulled away from the control tower at under 50ft after one dive.

Group asked us next day how much ammunition had been used against our attacker, and surprisingly we had pooped off more than any other station in the Group which had also been attacked that night. So we had all been caught with our trousers down, it seemed. But 4 Group had only once suffered from an intruder attack during the whole war, and had been lulled into a sense of false security, everyone concerned having got careless. From the AOC down to Base Commanders, Station Commanders, and the station defence officers. I kicked myself mentally for not having chased up my own defence officer to keep him on the top line, because it was my responsibility, and it was no consolation to know that others senior to me were equally responsible, or that several other Station Commanders had been caught out as well. And I was most unhappy at myself having let slip such a marvellous opportunity to knock an enemy intruder out of the sky.

My own defence major had no excuse to offer when I sent for him next morning to ask where the hell all the defence personnel had got to the previous night. But from then on they were all at their posts every time we took off or landed back from operations, with 50 per cent standing by at all other times as well. But of course it was too late. The Luftwaffe never came back again to repeat what had been a most successful operation for them, having shot down a number of bombers over our own bases at very small loss to themselves.

On 6 March, Wing Commander Dobson was posted to the Heavy Conversion Unit at Marston Moor on finishing a second distinguished tour of operations. His place was taken by Wing Commander G.B. Read, one of the first air gunners to be given an operational command. I had known him before too, he had done a full bomber tour, and was an experienced officer from an administration point of view also. The changeover therefore went smoothly. I myself was posted away on 14th March, to take an Air Disarmament Wing to Germany, so with the end almost in sight I was out of it. A pity in a way as I would have liked to have been with the chaps on 'VE' Day only seven short weeks ahead.

During those few weeks, the last stages of the heavy bomber campaign were to be fought out with the enemy fighting back to the last, incredibly hard considering the greatly reduced resources now available to them. The great day attacks on the Dutch sea defences to try and flood out the last pockets of Wehrmacht resistance in the strongpoints by-passed by the Canadian Army on their push into north-west Germany, and the smashing of Heligoland by a huge force of bombers, both took place.

Berlin, Nuremburg, and other targets in front of the advancing Russians were battered at night by strong forces, including the great attack on Dresden to help the Russian Armies, an attack much maligned by those latter-day 'liberal' Arm Chair Strategists perpetually sounding off from the safety and comfort of a freedom won for them by others at fearful cost in human life.

On 25 April 1945 the last bomber landed from the last operation. Bomber Command stood down. Their job done.

On 7 May, the war in Europe ended.

Epilogue

BOMBER Command was the only arm of any of the services to carry the war to the heart of the enemy with offensive operations throughout the whole war after the fall of France. Week after week after week, and frequently night after night continuously and relentlessly, the bomber crews prepared for and executed their dangerous missions. In spite of the fact that they knew their chances were pretty slim, their spirit, morale, and dedication remained magnificent throughout.

In Butch Harris's own words, the Command fought three separate and major campaigns, quite apart from the continuous and bitter strategic war of attrition which eventually involved 5,000 to 7,000 men being engaged in fierce air battles almost every night.

The first was a naval campaign, since the bombers immobilised, irreparably damaged, or sank, more submarines and warships, including capital ships, while in their harbours, than the Royal Navy itself did at sea.

Secondly, a land campaign which assisted the army. Because the bombing forced the enemy to concentrate on building night fighters and day fighters too once we were joined by the Eighth USAAF purely for the home defence of the Fatherland, they were thus unable to build up any tactical air force at all to protect their own troops, or to attack the invasion armies sent on to the Continent by the Allies. So we gave the Allied armies and our own tactical air forces complete air superiority over the battlefields from D-Day onwards. Thousands of the deadly German 88mm guns were also kept away from the battlefields on the ground because they had been converted to anti-aircraft use for home defence only – against the bombers.

Thirdly, by opening and keeping in action a Second Front long before D-Day itself. Germany was forced to deploy millions of able-bodied men and women for military and civilian duties to deal with the effects of the Allied bombers on the Reich heartlands. Fighter defence, searchlight and flak defences, rail and road and general bomb damage clearance, police and security services, and so on. Add to this the masses of guns, aeroplanes, ammunition, military equipment and stores of all kinds which would otherwise have been available for the Russian front, and the vast scale of our bomber intervention becomes apparent.

And little thanks we got from the Russians either. Or from our own government for that matter. Our crews were refused a campaign medal to acknowledge their great achievements in many costly air battles, and our C-in-C was not honoured with a peerage as comparable other war leaders were.

All the above is reflected in – and proved by – the official war casualty figures which follow. They are for missing and killed only, and do not include wounded or prisoners.

1. The Army – 177,850

2. Royal Navy – 51,578

3. The RAF – 76,342

These are for all theatres of war globally.

But out of the total RAF casualties of 76,342 no fewer than 55,573 were from Bomber Command alone, killed or missing in action while on bombing operations over enemy territory or killed on the way out and returning home from actual bombing missions!

No small wonder that what we used to say in jest finally turned out to be the bitter truth, that 'Only Owls and Bloody Fools Fly at Night.'

Enemy Coast Ahead

Guy Gibson

VC, DSO and Bar, DFC and Bar

Wing Commander Guy Gibson gives one of the most brilliant descriptions of the Dambusters raid by the Lancasters of 617 Squadron which he himself led.

256 pages, paperback 'b' format
photo section 0 907579 62 0 £5.99

Pathfinder

Air Vice-Marshal Don Bennett
CB, CBE, DSO

The autobiography of the leader of the Pathfinders – the élite force designed to carry out pioneering target-marking and precision-bombing of Nazi-occupied Europe.

272 pages, paperback 'b' format
photo section 0 907579 57 4 £5.99

Wing Aflame

Doug Stokes

The acclaimed biography of Victor Beamish, the legendary Irish station commander who flew an incredible 126 fighter sorties in the Battle of Britain.

224 pages, paperback 'b' format
photo section 0 907579 72 8 £5.99

Night Fighter

C.F.Rawnsley and Robert Wright

With John "Cat's-Eyes" Cunningham, "Jimmy" Rawnsley was half of one of the RAF's leading night fighter crews, destroying over twenty enemy aircraft.

256 pages, paperback 'b' format
photo section 0 907579 67 1 £5.99

Night Flyer

Lewis Brandon DSO, DFC and Bar

The exciting story of one of the most successful RAF night fighting partnerships of the war, the book also charts the development of night fighting.

208 pages, paperback 'b' format
photo section 0 907579 77 9 £5.99

Nine Lives

Al Deere OBE, DSO, DFC and Bar

The renowned autobiography of New Zealand's most famous RAF pilot who saw action from the Munich Crisis to the invasion of France in 1944.

288 pages, paperback 'b' format
photo section 0 907579 82 5 £5.99

Wing Leader

Air Vice-Marshal "Johnnie" Johnson
CB, CBE, DSO and Two Bars, DFC and Bar

The thrilling story of the top-scoring Allied fighter pilot of World War Two - 'Johnnie' Johnson.

320 pages, 'b' format paperback
photo section 0 907579 87 6 £6.99

Clean Sweep

Tony Spooner DSO, DFC

The remarkable story of Air Marshal Ivor Broom who rose from the rank of Sergeant Pilot to Air Marshal receiving the DSO, three DFCs, an AFC and other decorations along the way.

278 pages, 'b' format paperback
photo section 0 907579 18 3 £5.99

No Moon Tonight

Don Charlwood

A Bomber Command classic, this is the breathtaking story of a wartime bomber crew facing the nightly bombing of the most strongly defended targets in Nazi Germany.

224 pages, 'b' format paperback
photo section 0 907579 97 3 £5.99

Crécy Publishing Ltd,

1a Ringway Trading Estate,
Shadowmoss Road,
Manchester M22 5LH, UK

Tel: 0161 499 0024
Fax: 0161 499 0298
books@crecy.co.uk
www.crecy.co.uk